Solomon's Treasure

*The Magic and Mystery
of America's Money*

Solomon's Treasure

The Magic and Mystery of America's Money

By Tracy R. Twyman

Dragon Key Press
Portland Oregon

Dragon Key Press
PO Box 8533
Portland, OR 97207
USA

Visit us at
www.dragonkeypress.com

TABLE OF CONTENTS

PART I

Chapter One: Annuit Coeptis ... 3

Chapter Two: In God We Trust ... 9

Chapter Three: Plus Ultra ... 17

Chapter Four: The Almighty Dollar ... 27

Chapter Five: The Spirit of 1776 ... 35

PART II

Chapter Six: The Death of the West and the Birth of the Temple ... 43

Chapter Seven: The Renaissance and the Rise of the Merchant Class ... 51

Chapter Eight: The Empire in the East and the Church of the Holy Wisdom ... 57

Chapter Nine: The Head of Prophecy and the Aegis of the Goat ... 63

Chapter Ten: A Contract With Baphomet ... 73

PART III

Chapter Eleven: The Temple of Money ... 87

Chapter Twelve: The Iniquity of Priesthood ... 93

Chapter Thirteen: A Trespass Offering ... 97

Chapter Fourteen: The Shekel of the Sanctuary ... 101

Chapter Fifteen: King Solomon's Temple ... 117

Chapter Sixteen: King Solomon's Treasure ... 125

Chapter Seventeen: Solomon's Pact with the King of Demons   129

Chapter Eighteen: The Universal Agent   137

Chapter Nineteen: The Plot to Rebuild the Temple   141

Chapter Twenty: The Beautiful One   145

Chapter Twenty-One: Triskadekaphilia   147

PART IV

Chapter Twenty-Two: Spiritual Pyramid Schemes   159

Chapter Twenty-Three: The Law of the Harvest   161

Chapter Twenty-Four: Alchemical Miracles   165

Chapter Twenty-Five: A Commerce of Souls   169

Chapter Twenty-Six: A Mason's Wages   171

Chapter Twenty-Seven: The Mark of a Master Mason   175

Chapter Twenty-Eight: The Shekel-to-Dollar Exchange Rate   181

Chapter Twenty-Nine: Solomon's House - The New Republic   183

Chapter Thirty: A Final Thought   191

APPENDICES

Appendix A: The Tessera Hospitalis   195

Appendix B: The Wedjat Eye   199

Appendix C: The Bohemian Connection   203

Appendix D: Goat Money   **207**

Appendix E: The Jack in the Box   **211**

Appendix F: Casting a Fortune   **213**

Appendix G: The Root of All Evil   **215**

Appendix H: The National Treasure   **219**

Bibliography   **221**

PART I

Chapter One:
Annuit Coeptis

It is commonly known now, more so than ever before, that the United States of America was founded largely by men with a philosophy grounded in the occult: namely the members of Freemasonry, and other secret societies, who saw in the US a potential "New Atlantis" or "New Jerusalem." They foresaw the future of the United States as a beacon to the rest of the world, guiding the nations towards the formation of a New World Order of peace, democracy, and enlightenment. Many people today would agree that the US is indeed, in several ways, fulfilling this role already. If nothing else, most people would certainly agree that the America has come to dominate the world financially, and that among world currencies, the American dollar is king.

But what few people understand is the correlation between the esoteric doctrines of Freemasonry upon which the United States was founded, and the economic principles that underpin the American economy. Few understand that the dollar is a unit of magical energy, and the dollar bill itself a magical talisman. Although many words have been written by conspiracy theorists analyzing the Masonic symbols on the one dollar bill, no one has yet been able to sufficiently explain why these symbols are there, or what they really mean. Certainly no researcher yet has successfully connected the markings on American money to the hidden secrets of the American monetary system.

The symbolism of the American dollar bill has been the subject of Masonic conspiracy theories since the modern version was first rolled our during the Roosevelt administration in 1935. Masonic and mystical symbolism has been used on American currency since the very beginning, and was employed as a means of distinguishing our money from that of Old World Europe, which invariably featured the bust of the reigning monarch. In contrast, America's founding fathers agreed that American money should be decorated with the symbols of the anti-monarchist, pro-democratic Enlightenment philosophy upon which the Republic was founded, and many of these ideals were Masonic in origin. The Great Pyramid, the All-Seeing Eye, and quirky phrases like "Mind Your Business" appeared on early American currency. Indeed, the heads of "dead Presidents" and other state figures were not shown on US money until the twentieth century, when it was seen as less taboo. But all researchers of the subject agree that nothing tops the modern American one dollar bill for the sheer exactness and complexity of its mystical symbolism. The meaning of the symbolism is so deep, the metaphors so multi-layered, and each element so precisely placed, that although several of the other American bills have changed their appearance to prevent counterfeiting (with the heads moved off-center, and the addition of funky rainbow colors) the perfection of the one dollar bill has remained intact.

When analyzing the symbolism of the one dollar bill, most researchers tend to focus on the repeated use of the number 13, which they always insist is "an important number sacred to Freemasons", without demonstrating any proof of the supposed Masonic affinity for this particular number. This is, of course, the number of colonies that originally constituted the United States of America, and thus thirteen stars have been used in American heraldry since the start of the union, appearing not only on our first national flag, but upon many of our early coins as well. Since Freemasons were responsible for both the foundation of many of America's institutions and the design of our national symbols, it is tempting to ascribe a Masonic significance to the use of this number, and indeed there may be one. But there is no special mention of the number 13 in any known Masonic ritual, except perhaps in the rites of the Noble Order of the Shrine, where this number seems to be mentioned often, but with no particular meaning given to it. In any case, the Shriners did not exist at the time of the founding of the American republic. None of the quintessential Masonic tomes, such as Albert Pike's *Morals and Dogma*, make any special note of the number. Although Pike examines the meaning of many numbers in terms of cabalism and sacred geometry, mention of 13 is conspicuously absent, almost like an office building from the early twentieth century in which the thirteenth floor has been superstitiously omitted.

Even Freemason Manly P. Hall, in his 1944 book *The Secret Destiny of America* (where he interpreted the history of the United States as the unfolding of an ancient Masonic plan) could only offer lamely that 13 symbolizes Jesus and the twelve apostles, or the Sun and the twelve zodiac signs. One would expect him to offer something more interesting, but perhaps he was just being coy. Indeed, if there are any Masonic teachings regarding this number, then they are among the few Masonic teachings that have actually remained *secret* throughout the centuries. My research tends to indicate that there is in fact a proto-Masonic significance to this number, and one which would have been of special importance to the founders of the United States, had they known about it. I shall discuss this possibility in due course.

At any rate, Masonic or not, the number 13 is undeniably the most omnipresent, most repeated symbol on the one dollar bill, although its use is not always explicit. Most of these examples are found on the back of the bill. The pyramid on the left has thirteen layers, not including the eye at the top. Above the head of the eagle on the right, there is a constellation of thirteen pentagonal stars, arranged in the shape of a six-pointed. There are thirteen leaves on the olive branch in his right talon, and thirteen "Jonathan arrows", as they are called, in his right. There are thirteen horizontal divisions on the eagle's shield, and thirteen vertical ones. The motto "E Pluribus Unum", written on the banner in his beak, contains thirteen letters. So too does the motto "Annuit Coeptis", written above the pyramid on the left. Furthermore, if you add the number of letters in "Novus Ordo Seclorum" and "MDCCLXXVI" ("1776" in Roman numerals) written below the pyramid, you get 26, or two sets of thirteen. On the front of the bill, at the base of the portrait of George Washington, on each side there are eight leaves and five berries, indicating another two sets of thirteen. There are also thirteen stars on the chevron on the seal of the Treasury Department that is featured to the right of Washington, overlaying the word "ONE."

Clearly these allusions to the number thirteen are no accident. This truth is compounded by the letters in permanently featured words on the front of the dollar bill (that is, words not contingent upon any changing circumstance, such as the name of the US Treasurer). These words include: "FEDERAL RESERVE NOTE"; "THE UNITED STATES OF AMERICA"; THIS NOTE IS LEGAL TENDER FOR ALL DEBTS PUBLIC AND PRIVATE"; "WASHINGTON, D.C."; "ONE"; "TREASURER OF THE UNITED STATES"; "SECRETARY OF THE TREASURY"; "ONE DOLLAR; and "WASHINGTON." The total number of letters in these words is 169, or 13 squared.

Returning to the back of the bill, there would appear to be exactly *thirteen* examples of the use of the number 13 there. But in order for this to be correct, you have to count "IN GOD WE TRUST." Of course, there are only twelve letters in this phrase, but occupying the same space in the center on the back of the bill is the word "ONE", implying that we should add 1 to this sum and make 13. In addition, there are, on the front of the bill, four 1s at the corners of an inner rectangle on the front of the bill that is exactly thirteen centimeters long.

These 1s are part of a larger pattern, for in addition to the repeated use of the number 13, the number 1, or the word "one", is used profusely, much more than necessary to identify the denomination of the bill. The concept of "unity" could in fact be said to be the real underlying theme of the one dollar bill. And rightly so: it represents, after all, the original unit of currency upon which the American economic system is founded. It is the blueprint upon which all other dollar bills are based, and when we think of the American dollar, the first image that pops into our minds is the one dollar bill. As the official representation of the original *unit* underpinning the economy, its unity is expressed with the plenteous use of "1", the central placement of "ONE" on the back of the bill, and the use of the motto "E Pluribus, Unum" ("Out of Many, One") underneath a constellation of thirteen stars, representing the original colonies that were "unified" at the creation of the United States. The theme of "one" is continued with the use of the first American President, George Washington, on the front of the bill, and with the word "ONE" written next to him. As well, I would include the symbol of the pyramid on the back, which according to the designers of this emblem, was meant to represent the ideal state, made up of individuals (the stones) unified into one structure (the pyramid), under the divine unifying principle (the All-Seeing Eye of Providence).

Other strange features include the words "Annuit Coeptis" ("He [meaning God] favors our undertaking") and "Novus Ordo Seclorum" ("The New Order of the Ages"). These are both based on quotes from the Roman poet Virgil, although they have been slightly altered, and both quotes referred in their original context to "Juppiter Omnipotes" ("Omnipotent Jupiter"), essentially the Roman equivalent of the Judeo-Christian Almighty God. (Interestingly, "E Pluribus Unum" is also a quote from Virgil slightly altered, and some see in these alterations a numerological significance.) In the original Virgil poem, the words "Juppiter Omnipotes, Audacibus Annue Coeptis" were a plea for the deity to "favor my daring undertakings." The words on the back of the dollar bill not only plea for, but confidently declare, God's favor upon the "daring undertaking" there represented: the creation of a "New Order of the Ages", or new global power structure, headed by the newly-created republic of the United States. For these symbols and words belong not just to the dollar bill. They are part of the Great Seal of the United States, created in 1776, at the same time the nation was founded. It is the front and back side of the Great Seal which is represented on the back of the dollar bill.

The design of the Great Seal has never been ascribed to any one individual, and it has evolved a bit over the years. But the essentials of the design were sketched out right at the beginning, in 1776, the year of the Revolution, emblazoned in Roman numerals beneath the pyramid on the back of the seal. That's right: the roundel featuring the eye above the pyramid is actually the reverse side of the Great Seal, and the roundel featuring the eagle is really the front. It is the front of the Seal which is used to seal official US documents, not the back.

Several people are known to have contributed to the design of both sides of the Seal, including Benjamin Franklin, Thomas Jefferson, William Barton, Charles Thomson, and Pierre Eugene du Simitiere, and all but one were Freemasons. The first metal die for the Seal was cut by Robert Scot, a Freemason, in 1782. However, although dies were commissioned for both the front and the back of the Seal, only the front was actually cut. None was made for the back of the Seal until much later, and most people were not aware that their national Seal had a back to it at all until it appeared on the dollar bill in 1935. Thirty-third degree Freemason and historian Manly P. Hall wrote that the reverse of the seal was not originally used, "because it was regarded as a symbol of a secret society and not the proper device for a sovereign state."

Just like the Great Seal, the one dollar bill was also designed by a group of Freemasons working for the government; in this case, President Franklin Roosevelt, Secretary of Agriculture Henry A. Wallace, and Secretary of the Treasury Henry Morgenthau, although the design was executed at the Bureau of Engraving and Printing (which employed exactly *thirteen* engravers). It was Wallace's suggestion that the front and back of the Great Seal be used on the reverse of the dollar, although he originally wanted the front of the seal to be on the left, and the back of the seal to be on the right, which makes sense logically. But it was President Roosevelt who suggested switching that order, and putting the more interesting reverse of the seal on the left, which made more sense intuitively, since the Western eye naturally reads words and images from left to right.

"In God We Trust" was not placed on the bill until 1957. However, it was originally made the national motto of the United States in 1863 at the suggestion of Treasury Secretary Salmon P. Chase, who himself had supposedly been prompted to do so by a protestant minister concerned with the waning of religious fervor in the American public. This man purportedly wanted to ensure that the US would always be officially grounded in faith in divine Providence, and thus this motto was put on all American coins ever since, although it did not appear on paper currency until much later. But "In God We Trust" is indeed a Masonic motto – one used in almost all Masonic rituals, in which the participants must pledge to always put their "trust in God" during the ceremonies – and this specific phrase can be found in Masonic dictionaries. Its appearance on the dollar bill in the 1950s may have been meant to bolster a currency increasingly dependant on faith due to changes in American monetary policy.

Chapter Two:
In God We Trust

Major changes to the very nature of American money began in the 1930s, right around the time that the new one dollar bill was being designed. In an effort to help America climb out of the Great Depression, Roosevelt began employing the economic policies of advisor John Meynard Keynes, who suggested that, during times in which the private sector was not producing enough investment to stimulate the economy, the government should become the investor, financing public works, and dumping money into the system in whatever way possible to grow the economy. Thus Roosevelt instituted the "New Deal", creating an "alphabet soup" of bureaucracies, many of which have now become mainstays of federal government. Among these was the FDIC, or Federal Deposit Insurance Corporation, which insured bank accounts to a limited amount in the event of a bank's failure – something that was necessary after a number of bank failures had occurred in the previous years.

It may not be an accident that "FDIC" implies the word "fiducial", a financial term with its roots in the Latin word "fides", which means "trust, confidence, reliance, credence, belief, faith…. credit." Fides was symbolized in the Mithraic mysteries by two hands clasped together, now a common Masonic motif, and the logo of Allstate insurance. Coins whose face value is more than their metallic content are called "fiduciary tokens" because they require faith to be of value. For similar reasons, "trust" is a financial term that can mean, according to *Webster's Dictionary*, "confidence in the certainty of future payment for property or goods received"; or, "a fiduciary relationship in which a trustee holds title to property for the beneficiary"; or even, "any large corporation or combination having monopolistic or semi-monopolistic control over the production of a commodity or service."

But it was "faith" and "trust" in the American dollar that Roosevelt and his friends were attempting to create with the new design of the dollar bill. That faith was sorely needed, for in order to free up the money needed to finance the New Deal, Roosevelt had to institute sweeping changes to the country's monetary policy. He removed the dollar from the "gold standard" to which it had been implicitly set, so that he could have the money supply greatly expanded with no predetermined limit. It worked to stabilize the economy just in time for the United States to enter WWII, which turned out to be another great economic stimulator.

As part of removing the gold standard, Roosevelt had laws passed forcing US citizens to give all of the gold and silver that they owned to the government, in exchange for an equivalent amount of paper dollars. Americans' faith in the new system was severely tested the following year when the government devalued the dollar relative to gold, thus causing all who had made the exchange to lose 41 percent of the value of their money.

On July 22, 1946, at the end of WWII, an agreement was signed at a conference between 44 nations in which the other countries agreed to value their currencies in relation to the dollar, rather than gold, silver, or anything else. The US then set the value of the dollar at $35 per ounce of gold, and agreed to redeem dollars held by the central banks of other nations in gold upon demand. However, this led to a steady loss of US gold reserves, until finally, in 1971, President Richard Nixon closed the "gold window", announcing that the holdings of foreign central banks would no longer be redeemed for gold by the US government.

This was the final step in abandoning the gold standard. Now the value of the dollar floats freely in relation to foreign currencies, with no fixed standard of value. The value can only be manipulated by the market forces of the economy, and by the actions of the Federal Reserve. The result has been rapidly expanding inflation, which began during the Nixon years, and which has been felt by all the foreign currencies that were pegged to the dollar. Many of these currencies have repeatedly failed, and the governments of their countries remained continually insolvent, ever since.

So the dollar that we now use is one backed entirely by faith alone – the public's faith in America's economy, and America itself. The economies of other nations are dependant upon this faith as well. For if no one believed in the power of the dollar – if it was not universally accepted as a form of payment – then it would have no value. As Jack Weatherford writes in *The History of Money*:

The government will not redeem a dollar bill for anything other than another dollar bill. The dollar is simply fiat currency. The dollar rests on the power of the government and the faith of the people who use it – faith that it will be able to buy something tomorrow, faith that the US government will continue to exist and to accept dollars in payment of taxes and pay them out in expenses, and faith that other people will continue to believe in it. Aside from that faith, nothing backs up the dollar.

Likewise, William Greider wrote in *Secrets of the Temple: How the Federal Reserve Runs the Country* that:

Above all, money [is] a function of faith. It [requires] an implicit and universal social consent that [is] indeed mysterious. To create money and use it, each one must believe, and everyone must believe. Only then [do] the worthless pieces of paper take on value. When a society [loses] faith in money, it [is] implicitly losing faith in itself... The money process... [requires] a deep, unacknowledged act of faith, so mysterious that it could easily be confused with divine powers.

Of course, even before paper money became widely used, the worth of gold and silver coins rested on a similar social contract – a common, agreed-upon value. The difference is that gold and silver have intrinsic value, and when these coins were used in the past, their value was roughly equal (when made properly) to the value of the metal of which they consisted. But our current paper dollars are "fiat currency" – representations of wealth that have no physical existence until they are used to purchase something that does – in which case, they cease to be dollars.

The use of paper money was not new to America in 1935. They have been used throughout our history, beginning with the "Continentals" which financed the Revolutionary War. These were backed with nothing more than the promise that America would win the war, and begin collecting taxes from its citizens. A similar gamble was taken during the Civil War, which was financed by "Greenbacks", forebears of the modern paper dollar. In addition to these two currencies, each of which were issued by the federal government, there were, throughout the United States' early history, many paper dollars in circulation that were issued by privately-owned banks throughout the various states. These dollars differed widely in appearance from one another, which led to massive counterfeiting, and when the banks failed, which they often did, the dollars became worthless. Numerous measures were taken by the federal government in attempts to control this problem. Finally, in 1913, a series of banking collapses inspired the creation of the nation's new central bank, the Federal Reserve, and a new banking and monetary system, the Federal Reserve System.

The Federal Reserve is now the United States' national bank, and it is both quasi-governmental and privately-owned. It sets the basic operating policies for all of its member banks (which is most of the banks in the U.S.), and provides them with their money supply. The process they use to supply this money, "fractional reserve lending", is not new. Its almost as old as banking itself. But when backed by a powerful dynamo like the Fed, which created tremendous faith in the integrity of the money supply, the new money system became an unstoppable force.

In fractional reserve lending, a bank can take the money from its depositors' accounts, and lend it out to various persons or institutions on interest. It can loan out the vast majority of the money deposited (say, 87%), leaving only a fraction (13%) in the bank's vaults. This fraction is called the "reserve", and it is the only "actual" money sitting in the bank, backing all of the various loans - the only money that is really ready to be withdrawn, should the depositors choose to withdraw from their accounts.

When the loans are paid back, the bank earns a profit from the interest. Thus, the bank has caused its depositors' money to multiply, and has kept the difference for itself, essentially creating money out of nothing. If the bank has loaned money to another bank or financial institution, that institution can then loan it out and create even more money out of nothing. Or they can loan it to a person or business who can use it earn more money by producing goods and services that are sold. This money is then spent into the economy again. Thus the money supply multiplies exponentially, and the economy itself acts as a money multiplier – a manna machine, in a way. Money can always be used to make more money.

Now since the Federal Reserve is the point of origin for this money, the load initially injected into the system is sometimes called "high-powered money", because it effects the whole economy. It is the (comparatively) tiny mustard seed which causes the rest of the money supply to grow. The interest rate which the Fed chooses to set for the money it lends determines how much money will be borrowed by other banks at that time, and also determines the rate that those banks will charge for loaning money. This is the primary way in which the Federal Reserve controls the money supply, and thus, as much as possible, the American economy. Too much money being loaned out (and thus created) leads to inflation, and too little leads to recession. When the Fed first loans it out to the member banks, the money is "created", and each time those banks lend it out, they are breeding more. As Martin Mayer writes in *The Fed: The Inside Story of How the World's Most Powerful Financial Institution Drives the Markets*:

... The Fed's actions were always and necessarily pretty small by

comparison with the effects desired, and their effectiveness was
explained by the operation of a 'multiplier' inherent in a system where
banks had to keep 'reserves' against some fraction of their liabilities.
The bank that received the Fed's 'high-powered money' might lend 90
percent of it, and the bank that received the proceeds of that loan would
lend 90 percent of that, producing deposits in another bank that would
lend 90 percent of that, etc...

It is no wonder, then, that some see the way in which fiat currency,
especially paper and electronic money, can be simply "created", as
nothing short of magic. In 1705, Scottish philosopher John Law wrote in
his book, *Money and Trade Considered with a Proposal for Supplying*
the Nation with Money, that he had discovered the "Philosopher's Stone"
of the alchemists, which could purportedly turn lead into gold, or dross
into something valuable. The key to alchemy, he said, was the printing of
paper money, and in 1715 he was hired by the French government to put
his theories into action. Law was put in charge of France's national
Banque Royale, as well as the Mississippi Company, which gathered
investments from French citizens to finance operations in French
Louisiana, promising the investors profit payments. He set up a paper-
passing scheme between the bank and the company, in which investors
could borrow paper money printed by the bank to invest in the company.
They were expected to pay back the bank in gold, while the company
paid their profits in the bank's paper money, which was supposedly
redeemable in gold. The whole scheme collapsed dramatically in what
became known as "the Great Mississippi Bubble", and Law fled in
disgrace, dying shortly thereafter. But his ideas went on to influence
German writer and Freemason Wolfgang von Goethe.

In Goethe's classic play, *Faust,* the title character and his teacher,
Mephistopheles (the Devil), gain the favor of the emperor by offering
him the secret of alchemy: how to create wealth by printing paper money.
Soon the emperor presides over a robust economy and a licentious,
materialistic people. But the currency eventually collapses, just as all the
Devil's creations turn out, in this play, to be illusions.

It is my belief that the Freemasons and other occultists who have been
responsible for creating the United States, designing the dollar bill, and
engineering our economy have understood the principles of alchemy, and
have purposely chosen to construct our economy upon these principles.
They are the principles of creating worth from worthlessness, and for
creating a large volume from a small one, using the power of faith. I
submit that the creation of money by the Federal Reserve, and its

exponential multiplication by the procedures of the banking system, is analogous to the creation and multiplication of gold in alchemy. The power of money to transform almost any thing or situation into another is similar to the alchemical power of the so-called "universal agent" or "Philosopher's Stone", and the act of turning paper into dollars is like turning lead into gold. The members of the Federal Reserve Board are in many ways like sorcerers, conjuring wealth seemingly out of thin air and distributing it at will to transform the American economy according to their desires. The dollar is "fiat currency", declared into existence by the central bank in a manner similar to the creation of the universe by the divine words "Fiat Lux!" - "Let there be light!" Fiat money (best exemplified by the American dollar) is perhaps the only thing that truly means nothing, and has no independent existence, except in relation to something else (i.e., what it can buy, or be converted into), and yet it is the most powerful force within the human sphere of life – like the "Azoth", or secret essence of life spoken of in alchemical texts. And if one examines the history of the dollar prior to the formation of the Federal Reserve in 1913, one could easily conclude that most of these magical principles were at work in the American economy from the very beginning.

As stated, this system depends entirely on a religious faith by the American people in the supernatural power of the dollar. The ability of the United States President and other elected officials to uphold and improve the economy depends largely upon their ability to manipulate the spiritual will of the people, in much the same way that a priest or a magician would, inspiring them to have faith in the value of the dollar. This faith is reinforced by the financial terminology currently in use ("trust", "fiducial", "credit", etc.), as well as by watchwords and symbols found on American money – not only on the bills and coins we currently use, but on those dating back from before the formation of the Republic. These objects thus act as magical charms, containing a unit of magical charge that is passed on from one person to the next, and multiplied as the money changes hands. They also act as tokens of communal trust in, and fidelity to, the dollar as an institution. The symbols and key phrases associated with it thus work to enchant the public into a mass hypnotic spell, in which the mind of each individual confirms the consensus belief in the power of a dollar, and its ability to multiply itself as it moves through the system. Every time a person spends a dollar, or accepts a dollar as payment, they are confirming their belief in the dollar, and using it to exercise their spiritual will.

Now the mysterious markings on the dollar bill can be understood. The words "In God We Trust" are meant to inspire faith in the dollar as a currency, and faith in the American republic. One should trust the dollar the way one trusts in God, for it is implied that God himself has chosen to favor the U.S. and, by extension, the dollar. This is communicated by the message on the reverse of the Great Seal, "Annuit Coeptis" – "He [God] favors our undertaking." The words "E Pluribus Unum" and the other twelve examples of "one" on the bill, along with the pyramid, remind us that our society is made up of various parts that are essentially united, and money is the great uniter, since it is the one thing that everyone in the country uses, and each dollar can continually be passed from person to person, potentially reaching millions. The spider web motif in the background of the bill's design illustrates how we are all connected through the web of commerce. The bald eagle on the front of the Great Seal looks a bit peculiar. Masonic expert Manly P. Hall claimed that it was meant to secretly represent the phoenix, the mythical bird which eternally dies and is reborn, and which is a symbol of transformation in alchemy. (Indeed, the original proposals for the design of the Seal *did* call for a phoenix instead.)

Even the green color of U.S. dollars is symbolic, representing fecundity, plenteousness, and growth. Former U.S. Treasurer Mary Ellen Withrow explicitly stated in an interview with *New Yorker Magazine* that this is why the color green is used. This too is the reason why there is foliage all over the one dollar bill, including olive branches, oak leaves, laurel wreaths, and holly. But there have been representations of vegetation all over American money since colonial times, including corn, cotton, wheat, and tobacco. In fact, wheat is one of the most commonly depicted motifs on money from throughout the world and throughout the history. It was even on the first coins ever minted, as I will explain later on.

For now, though, we will examine the role that the Freemasons have played in the foundation of America, the ancient plan for the colonization of the continent, and the role that money played in the formation of the Republic. This will lead us to a greater understanding of the magic at the heart of the dollar.

Chapter Three:
Plus Ultra

As discussed in the previous chapters, members of Freemasonry and other secret societies were largely responsible for the settlement of North America, the American Revolution, and the formation of the United States.

But the plan to create a Masonic utopia in North America started much earlier. In fact, it started before the Order of Freemasons was officially founded, in the early to mid-seventeenth century (the exact date is not certain). Freemasonry has its roots largely in a medieval order of warrior-monks called the Knights Temple, who fought for Europe during the Crusades. I will get into the subject of the Templars at length later on, but for now it will suffice to say that the Templars are believed to have possessed an esoteric wisdom doctrine, and a secret goal of creating their own "philosophic empire" in the West, based on this doctrine. This put them at odds with the existing powers: the Catholic Church, and the ruling houses of Europe. They paid heavily for it, and the Order was suppressed in 1307.

The Templar leadership consisted of a close-knit group of noble families, who continued the Order's tradition after it was disbanded. One of these families was the Sinclairs, or Saint-Claires, of France and Scotland. The Sinclairs are purported to have been responsible for the development of an early form of Freemasonry in Scotland that was heavily steeped in Templar tradition. They commissioned the building of the elaborately-decorated Rosslyn Chapel in Scotland, which became "Lodge Number One" for this proto-Masonic fraternity.

One of the hereditary lords of Rosslyn was Prince Henry Sinclair, also called "Prince Henry the Navigator." In addition to belonging to a traditional Templar family, Henry could trace his roots back to the legendary Viking explorers whom historians believe may have explored North America long prior. Not only that, Henry was a member of the Knights of Christ, which was essentially a Templar spin-off groups, created by former Templars, with a focus on sea-faring.

True to his heritage, Prince Henry decided to do some exploring of his own, or so the story goes. He allegedly acquired a map of North America from a Venetian explorer named Nicolas Zeno. Then in 1398, Nicholas and his son Antonia, along with 200-300 soldiers, are said to have sailed in twelve ships to visit Greenland and the east coast of North America. It is from Antonio Zeno's son that we get the account of the voyage, as well as a copy of the map allegedly used. Nobody is sure if his account is true. However, Rosslyn Chapel was embellished with plant motifs of maize and aloe, which are native to the Americas.

In-between the time of Prince Henry's purported voyage and the formal establishment of Freemasonry, there were many proto-Masonic, neo-Templar groups working in Europe to continue the Templar tradition. They were also actively plotting to establish the Templars' dreamed-of "philosophic empire." There were groups calling themselves "Knights of the Rose-Cross", or "Rosicrucians." Other groups with different names nonetheless described themselves as having a "Rosicrucian philosophy."

The rose-cross is a multifaceted symbol with many layers of meaning. Certainly the Knights Templar had a red equilateral cross as one of their emblems, and thus could be called a "rosy cross." But the real rose-cross symbol actually showed a red rose at the center of a white cross, and specifically represented ancient, hidden wisdom. Like the Templars before them, and the Freemasons after, these "Rosicrucian" groups believed they were perpetuating divine secrets from the high cultures of antiquity: Greece, Rome, Egypt, Israel, Chaldea, and Persia.

This kind of knowledge had largely been suppressed, from the Dark Ages onward, by the Catholic Church, as well as by other Christian churches, and by the monarchs who depended on the support of these churches for their survival. But more than that, these existing power structures also actively suppressed the pursuit of new discoveries in science, new philosophies, and the expanding of human knowledge, for fear that the spread of such things would threaten their power. (Indeed, their fears turned out to be well-founded, for it was these ideas that ultimately toppled these monarchies and smashed the iron rule of the Church.) The Rosicrucians and proto-Masons believed that if a system of government could be set up somewhere that was not beholden to any church, or to any royal house, then its citizens would be free to learn these ancient truths and explore these new ideas. Then they could export their wisdom, and their enlightened form of government, to the rest of the world.

One of these groups was called the Order of the Helmet, to which belonged British aristocrat, lawyer, and philosopher Sir Francis Bacon. The "helmet" in their title referred to the plumed headgear traditionally worn by the Greek goddess Pallas Athena, whom they revered as a personification of wisdom. It is not known if this is the same secret society which Bacon went on to lead himself, or if he simply took inspiration from the Order of the helmet when creating his own fraternity. Nonetheless, he was the leader of such a group, the real name of which remains unknown to the public, but which has been cryptically referred to as "the Baconian Circle" by chroniclers. Some of the most influential and forward-thinking men in Europe belonged to this group, including Sir Robert Moray, who would become one of the main contributors to the development of Freemasonry.

Bacon himself was a prominent figure in Queen Elizabeth's court, and in English parliament. He was also one of the founders of, and a main stockholder in, the Virginia Company, which set up an English colony in Roanoke, Virginia. Some authors say that the colony was his idea, and that it was all part of the grand plan. According to Masonic scholar Manly P. Hall in *The Secret Destiny of America*:

The English program [of colonizing America] was under the direction of Sir Francis Bacon, and it was his genius that gave purpose to the enterprise... he was the head of a secret society including in its members the most brilliant intellectuals of his day. All these men were bound together by a common oath to labor in the cause of a world democracy. Bacon's society of the unknown philosophers included men of high rank and broad influence. Together with Bacon, they devised the colonization scheme.

To understand Francis Bacon's ultimate vision for the new colony in America, we need only read the treatise he wrote on the ideal philosophic empire, a utopian fantasy called *The New Atlantis*. For anybody who does not know, Atlantis was, according to a legend recounted by Plato, a perfect "empire of the gods" that supposedly existed prior to the Deluge. Bacon saw the idea of a re-created Atlantis as the perfect metaphor to use for the kingdom of wisdom we wished to establish in America, with hopes that the form of government planted there would spread throughout the world.

To communicate these concepts, Bacon used a fictional devise. He descried sailors on a ship departing Peru, bound for China, who are accidentally blown off course, and wash ashore in a previously unknown land with an existing high civilization. The capitol of this land is a "Wise Man's City", as Bacon described it, called "Bensalem", or "Son of Peace." This word could also be interpreted to mean "New Jerusalem", and that would be appropriate, for in *The New Atlantis*, Bensalem is ruled by a society of "philosophers" called "Solomon's house, or the college of the six days work."

This last part referred to the six days God took to create the universe, according to *Genesis*. When applied to the group called "Solomon's house", the term "college of the six days work" indicated that these philosophers were engaged in the study of the very secrets of creation. In the words of William Rawley, who wrote the introduction to *The New Atlantis*, Solomon's house was "instituted for the interpreting of nature, and the producing of great and marvelous works, for the benefit of men…" The doorway leading to the headquarters of Solomon's house said the following:

The end of our foundation is the knowledge of causes, and secret motions of things; and the enlarging of the bounds of human empire, to the effecting of all things possible.

Manly P. Hall thought that Bacon's work inspired that of the colonizers of America during his lifetime, and afterwards, as well as the founders of the new republic. Furthermore, he felt that Bacon had correctly predicted how the U.S. would use trade to export the philosophic truths on which it was founded. As Hall put it:

…Bensalem maintained a trade with all parts of the world, but not for gold, silver, jewels, silks, spices, or any other material commodity; its merchandise was the Light of Truth. Among the nations it traded with was Atlantis, which was declared [by Bacon] to be the same as America.

The idea of comparing America to Atlantis is fitting, for Plato said that Atlantis was just beyond the "Pillars of Hercules", which marked the Straits of Gibraltar and, according to ancient thinking, the limits of possible sea travel. In fact, on the title page of Bacon's *New Atlantis* there was a graphic which depicted a ship sailing between two columns, presumably those of Hercules. The age of exploration and the discovery of America proved that there was indeed a world beyond the Pillars. For this reason the words "Plus Ultra", which mean "More Beyond" in Latin, were written on early Spanish silver dollar coins circulated amongst the colonists, these words accompanied by a depiction of the two columns. The Pillars of Hercules have been linked symbolically with the two columns that supposedly flanked the entrance to the Temple of Poseidon in Atlantis. They were represented by the two pillars outside the Temple of Hercules on the island of Tyre, which was the architectural model for the Temple of Solomon. Also, the two pillars outside of Solomon's Temple, named Jachin and Boaz, play a very important role in Masonic ritual.

The Latin words for the Pillars of Hercules were "Columnae Herculis", the "columnae" being the plural of "columna", meaning "column" or "pillar." This is further related to "columen", meaning "that which is raised on high." Is the basis for yet another Latin word, "columba", meaning a "dove" or "pigeon." Doves hold a very significant place in religious traditions from throughout the world and throughout history. They were the sacred companions of the Middle Eastern goddesses Semiramis and Ishtar, the Egyptian Isis, the Roman Venus, and the Greek Pallas Athena. In Judaism and Christianity they were associated with peace.

One reason for this is their association with the story of the Flood of Noah. According to *Genesis*, when Noah's Ark was perched atop Mt. Ararat, he sent out a dove to survey the land. When it came back with an olive branch in its beak, he knew that the waters had begun to subside, and that it would soon be safe to leave the Ark. (It is interesting, then, that the front of America's Great Seal does feature a bird, in this case an eagle, holding an olive branch.)

Another story involving a dove, this time from Greek myth, evokes many of the same themes. It is part of the saga of Jason and the Argonauts, sailing in their ship, the Argo, in search of the Golden Fleece. ("Argo" is related to the word "Ark.") Their ship was attempting to pass through the Symplegades, two rocks marking the passage from the Black Sea to the Mediterranean Sea that were continually smashing against each other. Jason, the pilot of the Argo, sent a dove through the passage to see if it was possible to make it across without getting smashed. The bird made it safely through with the help of the Pallas Athena, and afterwards so did the ship. Later on, the dove, named Columba, was placed in the sky by Athena as a constellation, where it forever guides the Argo, which was also made into a constellation. These two star clusters are often associated with Noah's Ark.

It is interesting that the continents of both North and South America were originally called "Columbia", after their supposed discoverer, Christopher Columbus. The name is retained in the name of the South American country of Columbia, the Canadian province British Columbia, the Columbia Gorge between the U.S. states of Washington and Oregon, and of course, the U.S. capitol, Washington, District of Columbia. Just like the Athena of the Greeks, the Marianne of the French, and the Britannia of England, Columbia became personified as the national goddess of the United States, depicted on numerous coins and government monuments. On early designs for the Great Seal of the United States, artist and Freemason William Barton had even included a depiction of Columbia holding a dove.

Now is there possibly a link between Columbia, Columbus, and Columba the dove? Well, the word "columbus" is simply a masculine form of "columba", and thus means "a male dove." Could the explorer have been given this name this because he was sent out by the king and queen of Spain to explore beyond the Pillars of Hercules in search of a new passage to India, just as the dove Columba was sent ahead of the Argo to seek passage through the Symplegades?

Many authors have suggested that Christopher Columbus was working under the influence of a secret society of neo-Templars or proto-Masons. Citing a 1937 book by Spyros Cateras called *Christopher Columbus was a Greek*, Manly P. Hall asserted that "the real name of Columbus was Prince Nikolaos Ypsilantis, and he came from the Greek island of Chios." This is in contrast to the common understanding that Columbus was Italian. It is also commonly believed that Columbus was, like most people in his time, illiterate. But Manly. Hall believed the exact opposite, writing in *The Secret Destiny of America* that:

All modern research on the life of Columbus tends to prove that he was not a man of humble station, poor, or uneducated... Columbus is emerging as a man of impressive personality with marked abilities as a leader and organizer and an excellent classical education.

It was taught in school that Columbus could not even write his own name, but rather signed his contract with Ferdinand and Isabella the way all illiterate people did in those days – with an "X." The truth, according to Manly Hall, is much different. His signature did contain the letter "X", twice in fact. But it went like this:

S

SAS

XMY

X POFERENS

This purportedly stood for a cipher which could be interpreted to mean: "Salvus Christus, Maria, Yosephus – Christopher" – the names of Christ, Mary, Joseph, and then his own. As Manly Hall put it, "The signature of Columbus composed of letters curiously arranged and combined with cabalistic designs, certainly conveys more than is inherent in the signature of a private citizen."

By this he means that Columbus was acting as the agent of a secret society, specifically the same "society of unknown philosophers", which he believed was later led by Sir Francis Bacon. Perhaps significantly, Bacon mentioned in *The New Atlantis* that in Bensalem there was displayed a statue of Christopher Columbus. A possible third connection between Columbus and Bacon can be found in Manly Hall's report that Columbus "was inspired for his voyage by Plato's account of the lost Atlantis and the records of early navigation to the West... Columbus sailed his little ships for a land which by the writings of ancient philosophers he knew existed.

Indeed, Columbus may have had direct, inside access to maps and records of the voyages of Prince Henry Sinclair to America. According to several sources, Columbus' father-in-law was, like Prince Henry himself, a member of the Knights Templar offshoot group, the Knights of Christ. Some sources even claim that Columbus' father-in-law was a captain on one of Henry Sinclair's ships, thus providing Columbus with direct, second-hand knowledge of how to sail to America. It may be significant that Columbus' ships sailed under banners showing a red cross on a white field, one of the symbols of the Knights Templar.

In addition to these possible influences, Manly P. Hall described a mysterious, unnamed stranger who purportedly influenced Columbus, and was present on his first trip to America. As Hall told it:

... in browsing among old records, I have run across a dim figure involved in the life of Columbus, a strange man who seems to have served the explorer in the capacity of counselor. Nothing very tangible has yet come to light, but it is hinted that this mysterious person accompanied Columbus on his first voyage. He was not included in the list of mariners. He did not return, but remained in the West Indies; beyond this, no further mention in made of him.

This person was, according to Hall, Columbus' "handler" and "controller", guiding him in his work on behalf of the "society of unknown philosophers."

So is it possible that, prior to his voyage, Columbus had already been tipped off about America, via a network of secret societies, and that it was not a passage to India he was seeking, but rather the "New Atlantis" later envisioned by Francis Bacon? A provocative passage from Ignatius Donnelly's classic, *Atlantis: The Antediluvian World*, seems to indicate this:

When Columbus sailed to discover a new world, or re-discover an old one, he took his departure from a Phoenician seaport [the island of Chios], founded by that great race two thousand five hundred years previously. This Atlantean sailor, with his Phoenician features, sailing from an Atlantean port, simply re-opened the path of commerce and colonization which had been closed when Plato's island sunk in the sea. And it is a curious fact that Columbus had the antediluvian world in his mind's eye even then, for when he reached the mouth of the Orinoco he thought it was the river Gihon, that flowed out of Paradise, and he wrote home to Spain, 'There are here great indications suggesting the proximity of the earthly Paradise, for not only does it correspond in mathematical position with the opinion of the holy and learned theologians, but all other signs concur to make it probable.'

In a similar vein, author Michael Howard writes of Columbus that:

... [he] believed when he landed in America that God had led him to the New Jerusalem.

The name "America" for the two Columbian continents is of ambiguous original. The common belief is that the word comes from the name of Amerigo Vespucci, an Italian mapmaker who created maps based on Columbus' "discoveries." Supposedly the continents were named by accident when people mistook Vespucci's signature on the map to be a place-name. However, other authors have suggested that it was no accident at all. Prior to being hired for exploration by Ferdinand and Isabella of Spain, Columbus had been under the employ of King Rene d'Anjou, the duke of Lorraine in France. His family was highly connected to the old families of the Knights Templar, and to the esoteric circles that would eventually evolve into Freemasonry. Vespucci was employed by d'Anjou for a time as well, and it was at King Rene's salon in Sion-Vaudemont where atlas books containing Vespucci's maps were produced. The editor of one of these atlases wrote in it that the newly-discovered continents *should* be named after Amerigo Vespucci. Author John Noble Wilford, in *The Mysterious History of Columbus*, suggests that Columbus may have found America with inside information provided by Rene d'Anjou, and that the editor of the atlas may have named the place after Vespucci in order to deny Columbus credit for the discovery. In this version of the story, d'Anjou was angry at Columbus for using the information about America to benefit a rival royal bloodline, the Hapsburgs of Spain.

However, some authors believe that the word "America" has nothing to do with Amerigo Vespucci, but rather that it is a word with a hidden meaning known only to the secret societies that settled the continent. In 1895 the magazine *Lucifer*, published by H.P. Blavatsky's Theosophical Society, ran an article alleging that the name came from a native Peruvian word "Amaruca", meaning "Land of the Plumed Serpent", a reference to the tall, white, bearded man-god whom native South American legends say brought civilization to the continent in antediluvian times. Manly P. Hall also believed that this was the origin of the word "America."

But more contemporary Masonic historians, Christopher Knight and Robert Lomas, have postulated in their book *The Hiram Key* a quite different origin for the word "America." They connect it to the Mandeans, a Middle Eastern Gnostic sect influenced by the teachings of John the Baptist. The Mandeans were also connected with the Nasoreans, or "Qumranians", whom Knight and Lomas believe were responsible for depositing numerous secret scrolls beneath King Herod's Temple in Jerusalem (built on the foundations of Solomon's Temple.) Knight and Lomas believe that these scrolls were later discovered by the Knights Templar.

In the writings of the historian Josephus, it was recorded that the Mandeans believed that good people went to Paradise after death, to a land located West, beyond the ocean, and which was marked by a star called "Merica." The authors speculated the following:

We knew the Mandeans were the direct descendants of the Nasoreans, who we had also established were the same group as the Qumranians, the people who buried their sacred scrolls under Herod's Temple. It follows that if the forefathers of the Mandeans were the authors of the scrolls which the Templars unearthed, the mystical land beneath a star called 'Merica' might have been recorded in their secret writings. In short, it seemed possible that the Templars learnt about a wonderful land beneath the bright lone star 'Merica' from the scrolls, and if so, there is a strong possibility they sailed west to find it.

Whatever the case may be with regards to the origin of the words "Columbia" and "America", it seems fairly obviously that their development was not accidental. Perhaps the "mer" in "America" refers to the sea, as this syllable is part of the word for "sea' many languages. "America", then, may essentially mean "land beyond the sea", the "Plus Ultra" past the Straights of Gibraltar. This root syllable is also part of the word "mercantile", originally referring to the traffic of goods by ship. It was mercantilism hat quickly made America wealthy, prosperous, and dominant throughout the whole world. First, the discovery of the land beyond the pillars made the monarchs of the Old World rich. Then later, with the help of Freemasons, and with the development of the American dollar, the wealth would begin to flow in the other direction.

Chapter Four:
The Almighty Dollar

When Columbus discovered the Americas, purportedly while searching for a new route to India, he failed to acquire the vast quantities of silks and spices that he had been hoping to find in the East. However, the Spanish explorers who followed after him found that these "Indians" possessed treasures even greater than those of their counterparts in the East: voluminous hoards of silver and gold. To the natives, these metals were considered sacred because they were associated with the Sun and the Moon, whom they worshipped as gods. Thus, for example, the Aztecs and the Incas of Central America covered their religious temples and royal residences with gold, and there were statues and other artifacts made of gold to be found everywhere.

The Spaniards quickly and easily conquered these Indian tribes, seized their gold and silver artifacts, and made them into ingots which were shipped back to Spain. Within fifty years they had conquered all of the tribes and processed all of their treasure. They then began tapping Central and South America's rich mines, with the help of labor provided by the conquered natives, and this kept the treasure flowing back into Europe for almost another 300 years. The Portuguese, who also colonized the Americas, got into the business as well, and in 1695 began mining gold from Brazil using slaves imported from Africa. Between 1500 and 1800, it is estimated that about 165,000 tons of silver and 2846 tons of gold were shipped to Europe from the Americas, providing 70 percent of the world's gold output and 85 percent of its silver output. This was an unprecedented amount, and the sudden influx had an unprecedented impact upon the European economy. The first result became known as "the Great Price Revolution", where between 1540 and 1640, prices for goods and labor in Europe rose by 400 percent.

There is an economic rule that was little understood at this time: that whenever there is too much money chasing too few goods, inflation will occur. In this case, the silver and gold from America was minted into coins, which were used to buy goods and services on a previously unseen scale. This raised the demand for those goods and services, and thus, the prices. The more gold and silver there was coming into the continent, the less valuable it was. Many of the goods being purchased with these coins were imported from France, England, Holland, and the East, while Spain and Portugal had few goods to export in exchange. Thus much of the gold and silver left these countries almost as quickly as it came.

Yet for the rest of Europe, despite the inflation, the long-term economic effects of this sudden influx of coinage produced monumental changes in the structure of society. Before this, Europe was still shaking off the trappings of a feudalist society, with an economy based mostly on barter, although trade with coinage had been taking place with the help of Italian merchants, and before them, the Knights Templar, as I shall explain. At this time, many families still worked small plots of farmland owned by a noble lord to earn a subsistence living. They worked desperately each year to produce what they needed to eat, pay their taxes, pay their church tithes, pay their rent to their lord, and sometimes, through bartering, they were able to acquire other goods. Gold and silver coins were not being used by everyone. But after the colonization of America by Spain and Portugal, coins began to be used to pay for most things. This opened up the possibilities of economic exchange immensely. As Jack Weatherford explains in *A History of Money*:

The discovery of the great wealth of the Americas produced [an] immediate impact on the lives of common people... Professions that had traditionally depended upon money such as soldiers, artists, musicians, and tutors, now became even more focused on payment rather than on exchange of services such as room and board or rations paid in bread, alcohol and salt... Particularly in the seventeenth century, the new allocation of wealth gave rise to a middle class of merchants. They in turn spawned entirely new professions centered on money. As banking expanded, brokers appeared who specialized in the buying and selling of anything from real estate to shares in a trading voyage to China. Insurance men specialized in spreading out the risk of one voyage over many.

The result, more or less, of this influx of gold and silver was the creation of the merchant middle class. It allowed merchants and artisans to trade their goods more freely, to expand their overall wealth, and thus to buy not only more goods and services, but also land and titles. Newly wealthy merchants could even buy their way into a marriage with a lady from a previously impregnable noble class. It was the greatest stride yet in the direction of toppling Europe's old order in favor of the system that would eventually be called Capitalism. The success of Capitalism in the future would be largely attributed to the success of the American dollar. But the dollar was not originally an American currency.

In the year 1516, just five years before the Spaniards began looting silver and gold from America, Count Stephan Hieronymus Schlick discovered major silver deposits near his ancestral home in Jachymov,

Bohemia (now in the Czech Republic). His house, by the way, was called "the Castle of Joy", the same name given in the medieval Grail romance *Perlesvaus* to the Castle of the Holy Grail in which lives the fables Fisher King. Even more interesting is that the name of the title character in that story, Perlesvaus (also called "Perceval" or "Parzival" in other versions) supposedly means "pierce the valley", and it was in the valley of Joachimstal in Jachymov that Count Schlick discovered his silver. Schlick did indeed pierce the valley, and he began not only mining the silver, but minting it into coins as well. These coins soon began being circulated all over Europe, where they became known as "talers", after the "tal" or "valley" from which they were minted.

In 1527, Georgius Agricola was hired as the "mine physician" for Joachimstal. Agricola had spent his education studying alchemy – the supposed science of turning lead into gold, usually the purview of magicians and occultists. Over the years he had become frustrated with his studies, but, as Jason Goodwin writes in the book *Greenback*, "in Joachimstal… he saw something more interesting: incontrovertible proof that men could turn dross into silver. Mining, he decided, was what alchemy was meant to be." And although obviously mining had been practiced among civilized man since the earliest days of history, it had never been properly studied or written about in a scientific manner. Agricola's *De Re Metallica* became the first such treatise, and its author became known as the "Father of Mineralogy."

As the talers of Joachimstal began to spread, their name morphed into many different languages, and eventually the name "talers", or some derivation thereof, became the standard term for any large silver coin, especially in the Teutonic states. One taler, featuring the bust of Austrian Empress Maria Theresa, was issued in 1773, and became the most widely circulated taler in history. (Interestingly, Maria Theresa was married to the duke of Lorraine, the same title held by Rene d'Anjou, mentioned in the previous chapter as an employer of both Christopher Columbus and Amerigo Vespucci. The duke then became Holy Roman Emperor Francis I.)

This particular coin - the Maria Theresa dollar - was used all over the world, and was so loved that after Theresa's death in 1780, governments continued to have them made, bearing the date of her death, up until as late as 1975. Even after the Holy Roman Empire, which had originally produced the coin, was abolished in 1805 by Napoleon, and the mint that produced them was closed, Napoleon had the coins reissued from another mint, exactly as they had been, bearing the 1780 date, and the mint mark of the original mint. They continued to be made in the Austrian Republic until 1937, when the country was captured by Hitler's Germany, but Austria resumed making them between 1956 and 1975.

The Maria Theresa taler carried so much prestige that in some places, especially the Middle East and Northern Africa, they became synonymous with the concept of money itself, which is why Mussolini's Italian government was forced to begin minting them after they took over Abyssinia (now Ethiopia) in 1935. Belgium, Czechoslovakia, Russia, England, and India all produced these exact same coins in the post-WWII era. Such is the power of the "coin of the realm", to literally define reality. Both "realm" and "reality" have their roots in the word "real", meaning "royal" in Spanish and other languages. This is because the monarch defines what is "real" in his or her kingdom. As I have already mentioned, up until the creation of the United States, coins usually bore the face of the reigning monarch, and thus money became a powerful method for the monarch to remind his subjects of his ever-present influence. (This is still being done with British currency.) It was as though the monarch were putting his or her stamp of approval upon what was previously just a piece of metal, making it "real money." Every times a person uses the coin, he is transacting within the bounds of a system made "real" by the king's "rule." This connection is made explicit in the names of certain currencies, such as the Spanish "real", and the "rials" or "riyals" produced in Oman, Yemen, Saudi Arabia, and Qatar.

In 1497, not long after their hireling Christopher Columbus had returned from his first voyage to America, King Ferdinand and Queen Isabella the Spanish House of Habsburg had a coin issued called a "peso", the value of which was eight "reales." When the Spaniards opened a mint (soon to be one of the largest in the world) in Mexico, they began circulating the previously-mentioned coins featuring the Pillars of Hercules, and the words "Plus Ultra" ("More Beyond"). It was a lucky circumstance for the British colonists in America. For in the year 1695, the British government stopped exporting coins outside of its borders, even to its own colonies. Thus, the British colonists in North America were forced to acquire coins from the Spanish colonies in Mexico. The "Plus Ultra" peso became the most widely used coin amongst the thirteen British colonies, although they preferred to call them "pieces of eight" (referring to the eight reales they contained), or, more commonly, "dollars."

We can thank the early Scottish settlers in North America for the current name of the U.S. currency. Many of the early colonists were Scottish, eager to escape the direct English influence on the politics of their homeland. Many were also there because they had been expelled from the British Isles by the English government for being rabble-rousers and malcontents. These Scottish immigrants contributed greatly to the anti-British sentiment that began to develop in the colonies. Many of them fought in the Revolution, and contributed to the formation of the new republic. Of these, many were Freemasons, and Jacobites – that is, followers of the Masonically-aligned Stuart dynasty of Scotland. This family was directly related to Prince Henry the Navigator, a descendant of a family of famous Knights Templar, who purportedly sailed to America on a secret pre-Columbus mission on behalf of the Templar offshoot group the Knights of Christ.

In 1567, Scots Stuart King James VI commissioned the minting of the "sword dollar", so called because on the back it displayed the outline of a sword, a well-known motif of the Templars which often marked the graves of dead knights. In 1578, the same king issued a dollar bearing the image of a thistle, the symbol of his royal house. The Scottish royals chose to name their currency the "dollar", rather than the "Scottish pound sterling", as a challenge to the authority of the English monarchy. As Jack Weatherford explains in *A History of Money*:

The Scots used the name 'dollar' to distinguish their currency, and thereby their country and themselves, more clearly from their domineering English neighbors to the south. Thus, from very early usage, the word 'dollar' carried with it a certain anti-English or anti-authoritarian bias that many Scottish settlers took with them to their new homes in the Americas and other British colonies. The emigration of Scots accounts for much of the subsequent popularity of the word 'dollar' in British colonies around the world.

So in adopting the Spanish dollar as the American dollar, which the U.S. Congress did on July 6, 1785, the founders of America were being thoroughly *American*, because they were being anti-British. The U.S. did not establish its own mint until 1794. Even after that, since gold and silver were hard to come by, and the minting process expensive, the U.S. continued to circulate mostly Spanish silver dollars throughout much of the 1800s. So even though the U.S. did issue its own coins, the Spanish "pillar dollar" remained the "coin of the realm."

It is from the image on the pillar dollar that the dollar sign ($) is said by historians to have been derived, originally made with two slashes through the "S" instead of one, as is commonly done now. The reason for the supposed relationship is because on the pillar dollar the words "Plus Ultra" were written on banners surrounding each of the two pillars. So the dollar sign would then represent a pillar, or pillars, encoiled within a banner. This would then encompass, within a simple hieroglyph, all which is implied about America by the words "Plus Ultra" and the Pillars of Hercules – that America is the great New World dreamt of by the philosophers of old. The symbol is though to have been chosen for the dollar by Thomas Jefferson, who certainly would have understood its import. He also, according to Jason Goodwin in his book *Greenback,* chose for the dollar to be divided into 100 cents, and thus based on the decad, or ten, because he believed that this was the unit of measure used in pre-diluvian Atlantis.

Nonetheless, I think that there is more to the dollar sign than a representation of the Pillars of Hercules and an allusion to America as the "New Atlantis." I have always thought it to be reminiscent of the Caduceus, the magical wand of Hermes, a staff with a serpent entwined upon it, which has long been a symbol of alchemical transformation and healing (thus its use by the medical profession). Author David Ovason, in *The Secret Symbols of the Dollar Bill*, concurs, and adds that a symbol almost identical to the dollar sign is used in astrology to denote Mercury, the Roman version of Hermes, and the patron deity of alchemists.

There are other theories on the origin of the dollar sign. Modern Masonic scholars Christopher Knight and Robert Lomas, in their book *The Hiram Key*, note that the dollar was officially adopted by the U.S. on October 13, 1792, the anniversary of the arrest of the Knights Templar, and the same day in which President George Washington laid the foundation stone of the White House, in a Masonic ceremony, in a newly-adopted U.S. capitol, Washington, D.C. The authors then offer their own analysis of the meaning of the dollar sign:

...The 'S' was borrowed from an old Spanish coin but the two vertical lines were the Nasorean pillars of 'Mishpat' and 'Tsedeq', better known to the Masonic founders of the United States as 'Boaz' and 'Jachin', the pillars of the porchway to King Solomon's Temple.

This is an important detail, for as our study of the ancient secrets behind America's money progresses, we will find the pillars of Jachin and Boaz, as well as Solomon's Temple itself, increasingly relevant.

Chapter Five:
The Spirit of 1776

When in 1787, the U.S. issued its first coins, they were pennies, and they bore some unusual markings. On the front was a sun over a sundial, with the words "Mind Your Business", and "Fugio" (a Latin word meaning "I fly"). It was a reminder to be industrious, and to make good use of one's time, because time is money, and time (represented by the sundial), flies if you don't keep your nose to the grindstone. On the other side were thirteen circles linked in a chain, along with the words "We are one." We might not appreciate being chastised by our money like that in modern times, and perhaps people did not like it at the time, but within this morally self-righteous maxim, we can detect a hint of what would become the foremost trait of the character of the United States. It was President Calvin Coolidge who once famously said, "The business of the United States is business." And there can be little doubt that the dollar itself - the sheer power, and the overall stability of it - is largely responsible for America's success. In *Greenback: The Almighty Dollar and the Invention of America*, Jason Goodwin writes:

... the dollar seemed to do the work that class or creed did in Europe. It was America's bishop, its king, its squire. What Michael Chevalier in 1839 called a 'passion for money' was not a greedy passion, in the main: it simply reflected the importance of dollars and cents in a society that had no other standard to work on...

For the U.S. had only just emerged from an exhausting cycle of theological debate that rivaled in its way the acrimonious religious conflicts that battered Europe in the sixteenth century, and produced the nation state. America's theology was a secular one. It revolved around money and liberty, promise and return, profit and loss.

It revolved, in fact, around the miracle of money.

The money religion is known as the worship of Mammon, and the Almighty Dollar is the supreme being.

The idea of the United States, and the values inherent in American culture, have become almost synonymous with the idea of free market Capitalism. It cannot be a coincidence that the Declaration of Independence was signed in the same year that economist Adam Smith's book *A Wealth of Nations* was published, the definitive work on the laws and merits of a Capitalist economy. Smith came up with the idea of what he called "the invisible hand", his term for the sum total of the individual forces that, collectively, drive the economy, especially the needs and desires of the human individuals participating in the economy. In Smith's philosophy, the invisible hand guides the laissez faire (or free market) economy (output, price, and profit) towards the greatest common good as individuals act in their own self-interest to "pursue happiness" - that is, wealth, prosperity and comfort. (We should recall that the early drafts of the Declaration of Independence asserted the colonists' right to "life, liberty and the pursuit of property", where "property" was later changed to "happiness.")

 In Smith's book he noted that a merchant or artisan, out of a selfish motive for gain and profit, produces, not the sort of products he likes or enjoys necessarily, but what the public wants or needs: i.e., whatever is likely to sell. He sells that product at as high a price as he possibly can, again out of selfish motive. But the buying public has selfish motives as well. They will not pay more for the same thing when they can get it cheaper somewhere else, so the merchant can only charge as much as they are willing to pay. Supply and demand dictate that the needs of the public will always be supplied at the lowest price possible. Thus, by selfishly pursuing their own desires, everybody wins, and the Capitalist economy inherently works ever-increasingly towards the greatest public good. The investment of capital anywhere in an economy causes overall wealth (the, G.D.P., or Gross Domestic Product) to grow with no limit. As Smith writes, a man:

...neither intends to promote the publick interest, nor knows how much he is promoting it... he intends only his own gain, and he is in this, as in many other cases, led by an invisible hand to promote an end which has no part of his intention.

 Adam Smith's philosophy was, in a way, the economic outgrowth of Newtonian physics. It was part of the trend of "Enlightenment" philosophy that was sweeping the intelligentsia of Europe during the eighteenth century, although it had begun in the previous century with thinkers like Sir Francis Bacon, Isaac Newton, John Locke, Rene Descartes and Voltaire. It was based on the idea that the universe could be understood by the human mind, studied, quantified, and analyzed using reason and science, and that the whole could be comprehended by analyzing its parts. Indeed, "science", as such, had not existed previously, and philosophers (the closest equivalent to scientists) were simply expected to use their writings and studies to confirm the teachings of the Catholic Church. When the Protestant Reformation, and the creation of the Anglican Church, broke the absolute power of the Pope enough to allow freedom of thought to spread amongst the educated, this new "Enlightenment philosophy" was developed. Part of this worldview involved the somewhat naïve belief that human nature was inherently good, but that social institutions squashed this inner nature, and that if society were structured so that men could freely follow their natural instincts and desires, society as a whole would prosper. Adam Smith's economics were based on this presumption as well. Yes, man's instincts are selfish, but selfishness is inherently good.

These views formed part of the basis for the anti-monarchist, republican political movements that were spreading all over Europe, and it certainly formed the basis for the political thought of the founders of the United States. Enlightenment philosophy can essentially be considered Masonic philosophy, with much of the occult mumbo jumbo or traditional Masonic thought simply translated into modern "scientific" terminology. Certainly, much of the Enlightenment was fostered by the Royal Society, a body of scientists and thinkers founded by Sir Francis Bacon that was sponsored by the British government. A search through history books will confirm that most of the Royal Society scientists, and indeed, most of the Enlightenment philosophers, were members of either the Masonic brotherhood, or some similar offshoot. As Michael Baigent and Richard Leigh wrote in *The Temple and the Lodge*:

Without eighteenth-century Freemasonry, the principles at the very heart of the conflict – liberty, equality, brotherhood, tolerance, the 'rights of man', would not have had the currency they did. True, those principles owe much to Locke, Hume, Adam Smith and les philosophes in France. But most, if not all, of those thinkers were either Freemasons themselves, moved in Freemasonic circles or were influenced by Freemasonry.

So capitalism, as an economic philosophy, is an outgrowth of the Enlightenment era. But what does "capitalism" mean? The word comes from the Latin "capitalis", meaning "of the head", and the relation of this concept to the later financial connotation of the word "capital" is unclear. Its first use in that sense was actually the circa 1630 word "capitale", meaning "stock or property." The basic building unit of capitalism is the corporation, and these first started, not surprisingly, in the 1600s. The development of the corporation was spurned on by the improvement of sailing and navigation technology, and thus the boom of the shipping industry. This is why the root word "mer", meaning "sea" is at the heart of the word "mercantile", and why we still say "shipping" when we are referring to the transport of goods, no matter the method. The improvement of seafaring led to the blossoming of a new form of economy. Now merchants could sail to India, Asia, Africa, or even the Americas, and trade an unprecedented variety of goods, with an unprecedented volume of gold and silver coin available to aid those transactions.

But ships and crew were still expensive, and the voyages dangerous. If one trip went bad, an investor could find himself in debt for life, and worse, in debtor's prison. So the government of Holland, a leading power amongst the sea merchants of Europe, came up with a novel concept by which numerous merchants could pool their resources and minimize their individual investment risk. They created a "corporation": a group of investors who would collectively invest in a business venture to form a company, which then became a "legal person" according to a declaration in the company's charter, granted by the government. This "person" was then able to enter into legal contracts and business ventures, just like a regular person. Only there was one important difference: unlike a real person, the corporation could not be thrown into debtor's prison. Indeed, there was, and is still, no real way to force a corporation to pay its debts. When the corporation determines that it is no longer viable, it declares bankruptcy and, more often not, leaves those to whom it owes money holding the bag. This arrangement worked out well for the Dutch merchants of the seventeenth century, and soon the idea was picked up by other countries, like Britain. Thus the formation of the famous "British East India Company", as well as its rival, the "Dutch East India Company" was possible.

In a corporation, the total worth of the company is divided into "shares", which are sold to the investors as percentages of the company's worth – slices of the pie. The more shares each investor owns, the greater his slice of the pie. The price, or value, of each share fluctuates along with the overall value of the company. Dividends from the company's profits would be paid to the investors annually in relation to the number of shares that they owned. At any time, an investor may sell his shares to another investor. It did not take the Dutch merchants long to realize that these shares of a corporation could be traded almost as a form of currency, just like any fiat money. This led to the creation of the first stock exchange in Holland in the year 1631, a year after "capitale" began being used as a financial term.

Prior to the invention of corporations, the rise of capitalism was foreshadowed by a slow economic revolution that took place between the fifth and thirteenth centuries. This was a result of the aforementioned phenomenon of "mercantilism": the trade of goods overseas via the newly-developing shipping technology for the explicit purpose of turning a profit in coin, not merely to barter. This practice paved the way for capitalism, as merchants learned to buy goods in coin at one place and then sell them at a higher price somewhere else. Mercantilism originated in Rome and the Middle East, and was widespread throughout the Roman Empire. Indeed, the spread of the Roman Empire and the spread of mercantile trade were really one and the same process.

But when the Roman Empire fell, mercantilism fizzled. The economy of what was now Europe contracted and localized. This led to an overall decline in the use of coin for trade. As the "Dark Ages" took root, economics, education, health, and scientific progress came to a halt. The system of Feudalism began to develop, in which only the nobility had access to, or even need of, money. Everyone else worked small farms to produce what they and their feudal lords required.

Yet throughout Europe's Dark Ages, the cultures of North Africa, the Middle East, Asia, and even Islamic Spain continued their tradition of mercantilism, and continued to trade in coin. Not only that, while the Europeans were devolving scientifically (with the help of repressive Catholic Church policies), Middle Eastern cultures were developing newer, more sophisticated methods of sailing, minting coins, calculating money, and otherwise doing business. Europe would languish in its own ignorance until, in the eleventh to thirteenth centuries, an empire of enlightened warrior-priests would rediscover the secrets of the East, and lead Europe out of the dark, onto the path to the Renaissance. A large part of this involved the rediscovery of the power of money. I am speaking, of course, of the Knights Templar, forefathers to the brotherhood of Freemasons, and inventors of modern banking.

PART II

Chapter Six:
The Death of the West and the Birth of the Temple

The rise and fall of the Roman Empire mirrored the rise and fall of the Roman mercantile economy, and in fact, Rome's decline was largely caused by a decline in trade. It was the ancient Lydians who had first begun the minting of coins, but it was the enterprising Greeks who spread the trade of coins around the ancient world to all of the many nations with which they did business. The Romans, who succeeded the Greeks as the next great culture, took it even further. As the expanding empire conquered more and more foreign lands and appropriated them into their economy, they built what Jack Weatherford describes in *A History of Money* as:

...the world's first empire organized around money. Whereas the great Egyptian, Persian, and other traditional empires had largely rejected money in favor of government as the main organizing principle, Rome promoted the use of money and organized all of its affairs around the new commodity.

But this same process would eventually become their undoing. Like the Spaniards who would later appropriate American lands into their empire, the Romans fell into the same trap. Their conquests made them rich, but the decadent emperors rapidly spent their money importing luxury goods from these and other foreign lands. They purchased much, but they exported little, and thus Rome's wealth flowed in only one direction – out of Rome. To make matters worse, they now had a huge empire to maintain, which was expensive, and they also continued their military efforts to expand this empire, which meant hiring mercenary armies.

To pay for everything, one emperor, Nero, tried to increase the amount of money available by reducing the silver and gold content of the coins, and making them smaller. All this resulted in, of course, was inflation, and each of the coins was now worth less than it was before. To get more of these devalued coins into the government coffers, taxes were increased greatly, while welfare programs were devised to keep the poor from rioting. As any student of trickle-down economics will tell you, such actions stifle growth and discourage enterprise. But in the latter days of the Roman empire, the effects of this would forever alter the very economic system in which society operated. They slouched from a relatively free society with a free market and an open class system (with class defined by monetary wealth) towards a closed, repressive, and highly stratified caste system based upon the privilege of noble birth. As

John Weatherford explains:

Like people anywhere, once the tax burdens became too high in comparison to the benefits and services offered by the government, the Roman subjects found ways to avoid taxation. Commerce declined. People produced more of what they needed for themselves and traded less on the open market. While the poor suffered from heavy property taxes, the <u>latifundia</u>, the great landed estates, grew greatly, particularly those that had been granted a tax-free status. The high taxes induced more peasants to abandon their land and move to the tax-free estates where they at least had a steady supply of food and the essential goods produced on the estate itself.

In other words, society was slouching towards feudalism, which would soon become the West's new economic system. The way was further paved for a feudal state when Emperor Diocletian initiated laws forbidding farmers from selling their land, and dictating that all sons had to follow in the same profession as their fathers. Thus generations were locked into the same occupation on the same piece of land. Money all but vanished from society. The government was still minting highly-devalued coins for commerce, but refused to accept them as payment for taxes. Soon there was so little money around, and what there was inspired so little confidence, that the government found it had to conscript people into slavery to complete state projects. They also persecuted Christians within their domains, and appropriated what wealth they had.

Things took an interesting turn with the rule of Emperor Constantine from 306 to 337. It was he who, after experiencing a religious vision, converted to Christianity, and made it the new religion of the state. Some cynical historians choose to say that Constantine was just an opportunist who wanted to use Christianity for his own ends, and they say that he remained an unrepentant pagan who only "truly" converted to Christ on his deathbed. But to be specific, the cult that Constantine remained loyal to was that of Sol Invictus, or "the Invincible Sun", in which the Sun was revered as a symbol of the omnipotent God. I submit to you that this does not a "pagan" make.

At any rate, Constantine contributed much to the historical foundations of Christianity. He issued the Edict of Milan in 313, which gave Christians the right to practice their religion freely, and returned their confiscated property. In 325, he convened the Council of Nicea, which developed the Nicean Creed, a major basis for all mainstream Christian thought today. Because of these things he gained the moniker "the thirteenth Apostle." He then proceeded to have many of the pagan temples of Rome looted for their gold and silver artifacts, which he melted down and had minted into coins. These he used to finance the building of a new, Christianized capitol in the East on the Black Sea, which he named after himself: Constantinople.

In doing so, he diverted all future investment and trade to the new capitol as well. This was the beginning of what would become known to historians as the "Byzantine", not the "Roman", empire (although the people of the new Eastern Empire still called themselves "Romanians" at the time). Byzantium continued to flourish, but the old Roman Empire collapsed. It was sacked by barbarians in 476, and thus began what was known as the "Dark Ages" of the West.

With no real money in circulation, Feudalism became the new economic system. From 476 until the emergence of the "Renaissance" (put by some historians at about 1350 B.C.), peasants worked on large manors owned by nobles, where every effort was made to keep the manor self-sufficient. On the manor, they produced their own food, clothes, and tools, and paid their taxes in these goods. Everyone lived and died on the same manor, just as their father had done before them. Reading, writing, math, and every form of learning or science virtually ceased. The only way to learn these things was to join the clergy, which is why the Catholic monastic orders became the new bastions of the intelligentsia. Because of their overall ignorance, people were reluctant to use money for trade, as most people did not know how to figure numbers at all. Learning and trade continued in the Byzantine East, but in the West, it was dead.

The only people who were lending out money at all in Europe were Jews. For many years, Jews had been banned from practicing any profession other than money-lending. This was not done just because Jews were "good with money." The Catholic credo held the lending of money upon usury to be sinful, but since Jews were already damned to Hell in the eyes of the Church, they were encouraged to take on the dirty job of money-lending for the rest of the community. In England, William Rufus, son of William the Conqueror, forbade Jews from converting to Christianity, which, as Paul Morrison writes in *The Poetics of Fascism: Ezra Pound, T.S. Eliot, Paul de Man* , would "rid him of valuable property and give him only a subject." But when Jews were expelled from many communities, of and on, during the pogroms of the Middle Ages (sparked periodically, when people began to realize how much money they owed to the Jews), these communities lost their moneylenders.

  Luckily, however, the Holy See was inspired by God to grant the
Knights Templar immunity from this anti-usury injunction. As I
mentioned earlier, briefly, the Templars, or as they were officially titled,
the Poor Knights of the Temple of Solomon, were an order of crusading
warrior-monks thought to have been the lineal predecessors of the Order
of Freemasons. Formed in the early twelfth century, like many other
knightly orders which formed during the Crusades, they were an elite
fighting force of Catholic monks at the forefront of the European struggle
to capture and control the Holy Land. But in addition to fighting, they
were also in charge of fulfilling many practical roles for the community,
among them, money-lending. The Church allowed the Templars to
charge interest on loans at an even higher rate than Jews had been
allowed to. In fact, they were granted a charter that basically established
the Templars as a law unto themselves, accountable to no one but the
Pope. Thus they were able to operate autonomously at their various bases
throughout Europe. They even had the right to establish their own
sovereign country, which is essentially what they were doing in the Holy
Land when they helped to create the Latin Kingdom of Jerusalem.

  The Knights Templar had a very interesting entrance policy. Not only
did new initiates pledge lifelong membership in, and fidelity to, the
Order, but they also took very stringent vows of celibacy, secrecy, and
poverty. This last part was most interesting, for it amounted to the
ultimate entrance fee: one literally handed over everything one owned to
the Order, and vowed to remain in "poverty", donating any earnings one
might make after joining, to the Order as well. Considering that their
knights were taken from the cream of European aristocracy, the younger
brothers of wealthy and powerful heirs, this was quite significant. It
allowed them to amass a large amount of wealth and land in a relatively
quick amount of time.

  They then multiplied this wealth exponentially over the next several
decades by investing in various business ventures. They farmed,
manufactured textiles, built roads and hospitals, and engaged in all sorts
of trade. They were responsible for numerous technological advances
during this time, either through their own invention, or through
techniques that they learned through their frequent contact with Arabs,
Jews and Byzantines. Their business ventures had the effect of largely
transforming Europe's economy, paving the way for the mercantilism
that was emerge soon in post-Medici Italy, later giving birth to
Capitalism in Europe and America. The Templars' most significant

contribution on this front was in the field of banking, which became their most lucrative industry.

The Templars were, first and foremost, the official guardians of pilgrims en route to the Holy Land. This was supposedly the reason why the Order was created in the first place. In this capacity, they devised a system to protect pilgrims from the "highway robbery" that often made such pilgrimages dangerous. Instead of loading themselves down with gold and provisions, which were likely to be stolen, the pilgrims would simply deposit some money in the form of gold or silver at the Templar preceptory nearest to their point of departure. From there they would make their way to Jerusalem along a pre-selected route consisting of a series of churches and cathedrals, which were themselves associated with nearby Templar preceptories, each featuring banking services. There the pilgrim would present the banker with a "chit": a piece of paper that was encoded with ciphered information regarding the pilgrim's deposit at the originating bank. The pilgrim could then withdraw from the bank at his current location the amount of money he need to pay for his stay at that particular stop on the route, or make donations to the various churches, and could leave the rest in his "account." He could also make direct charges to the account for any goods or services which the Templars themselves were able to offer the pilgrim, which was often the case.

It is thus that the word "check" or "cheque" entered into the English and French languages. Indeed, a great many Middle English words, especially those pertaining to banking and commerce, seem to have originated in one way or another with the Templars. In the case of "cheque", it was related directly to the use of the chequerboard clothe which Templar merchants and bankers used to square their accounts – to "check" their assets and liabilities. The Templars had originally picked up the use of the chequer pattern from their contact with the East, from whence they also learned to play chess, and it is theorized by some authors that it was Templars who originally combined the chessboard (which was not at first chequered) with the chequerboard pattern, enhancing the deep symbolism that the game of chess already possessed. The use of the chequerboard as an abacus became widespread as mercantilism progressed, and thus the term "exchequer" came to mean "a treasury, as of a state or nation." The term "check" may be related to "jetton", which is the name of the round coins that were often used as tally chips on exchequer boards, representing various denominations of money. They were introduced by the Templars in France in the mid-thirteenth century.

But before we get to that, let me back up and explain. As the Templars expanded their banking empire, and as they came to control many other staple industries throughout Europe, they quickly became the continent's most dominant economic influence. Never before has a single institution used money alone to amass so much worldly power. This power threatened not only the monarchs of Europe (most of whom were now financially indebted to the Templars), but even Pope Clement V, who was no longer was able to hold the Templars under the thrall of his signet ring. Soon the Templars would become a force that no one could stop, and they seemed to hold allegiance to no one else either – no earthly power, at least. Their enemies hypothesized that for the Templars to have become so wealthy and powerful in such a short span of time, they would have had to have made a pact with the Devil. With a little investigation, it was discovered that in fact they had.

When the Templars were arrested en masse on Friday, October 13, 1307, on charges of idol worship and heresy, there were found throughout their preceptories various human skulls, and representations of human skulls or severed heads, which appeared to have been afforded certain ceremonial importance. The symbol of the skull and crossbones, apparently invented by the Knights Templar, was used everywhere throughout their possessions. Carvings depicting a grotesque goat-headed creature, with a semi-human body at once both male and female, were also found in the Templars' ritual chambers. In confessions painfully extracted, many knights admitted that the skulls, the heads and the hybrid creature all represented their secret god, "Baphomet", whom they worshipped because it "caused the land to germinate", and also "made them rich."

Modern occultists, for whom Baphomet is now a potent symbol, see in this idol a representative of the "Universal Principle", the "Azoth" or "Fifth Element" which to alchemists is the key to turning lead into gold. This is probably what it meant to the Templars too, as we shall see. But to their interrogators, the tortured knights were confessing Devil worship, and they were punished accordingly. The Order was disbanded, the Grand Master burnt at the stake, and the offending knights sent to do penance at various monasteries. The power of the Templars was crushed.

Chapter Seven:
The Renaissance and the Rise of the Merchant Class

After the disappearance of the Knights Templar, the tradition of mercantilism and banking continued on, conducted mainly by a group of Italian merchant families based in cities like Genoa, Pisa, Florence, Venice, and Verona. These families chose to get around the Catholic prohibition against usury by using semantics. Instead of issuing "loans", they wrote out "bills of exchange", specifically called "cambium per lettras" in Latin, meaning "exchange through written documents or bills." These bills were contracts in which the bank gave the contractee an amount of money in one currency, and that person agreed to pay the bank a certain amount of money in another currency at a certain date. It just so happened that the amount of money paid back had an exchange value greater than the amount of money that had originally been issued. Thus the Italian banks got their "interest" without having to call it that.

The new Italian bankers brought money-lending to a whole new level, because they brought it to the street. The Templars had dealt exclusively with the noble class, but the Italians dealt with everybody: landlords, merchants, and vendors, with no discrimination between Catholic, Muslim, or Jew. It was around this time that the word "bank" actually came about, from the Italian word for "table", or "bench." Unlike the Templars, who operated out of fortified castles, the Italian banks operated from temporary benches and tables set up at market fairs that took place in various cities throughout the year.

One of the advantages of this new system was that the economy was not bound to the availability of any single currency. In the past, a shortage of one type of coin could put business to a halt. But now, if there was a shortage of one type of money, the bankers would just continue working with another type. They could also continue to write bills of exchange representing a certain currency, even if there was not much available, so long as the currency still retained the public confidence. If there were not enough coins available in the currency in which the loanee was obliged to pay the bank, he could arrange to pay them in another currency instead.

Yet another advantage of this banking system was that now money was flowing much more freely in and out of bank accounts, and thus, being utilized much more efficiently. Instead of vast treasure-stores of money sitting stashed around in a castle, it was in a bank account, allowing the bank to use it as a reserve to loan money out to merchants or to other bankers. This money would then be used by the merchant loanees to do business, stimulating the local economy, and would eventually be paid back to the bank with the equivalent of interest. Thus each deposit into one of these banks multiplied the overall money supply of the economy exponentially. As Jack Weatherford explains:

Under the new system a bag of a hundred florins [gold coins from Florence] that might once have sat idle for years in a noble's strong-box could now be deposited for safekeeping in an Italian bank that had access to branches across the continent. The bank then lent the money and circulated the bill of exchange as money. The noble still had his one hundred florins, which were now on deposit in the bank; the bank had one hundred florins on its books. The merchant who borrowed the florins was richer, and the person who held the bill of exchange now had one hundred florins as well. Even though only one hundred gold coins were involved, the miracle of banking deposits and loans had transformed them into many hundreds of florins that could be used by different individuals in different cities at the same time. This new banking money opened vast new commercial avenues for merchants, manufacturers, and investors. Everyone had more money; it was sheer magic.

Of those who profited, none did more so than the banking families of Peruzzi, Bardi, and Acciaiuoli, all from Florence. Their wealth and money-lending services gained them influence with both the Papacy, and the monarchy of England (Edwards I, II, and III), whom they were largely responsible for financing. Because of these families, Italian currencies, especially the Florentine florin and the Venetian ducat, became the standard coins of continental Europe. The downfall of these families came when the English monarchy, then headed by Edward III, defaulted on its loans with the bankers in 1343. Soon there was no reserve cash left in the banks to cover all of the other loans that they had outstanding. The system worked great so long as all of the participants maintained their confidence in it. But now the vulnerabilities of a system built on faith were exposed, and these banking enterprises collapsed like a house of cards. An outbreak of plague in Italy from 1343 to 1348 finished them off.

Luckily for Europe, though, another family was soon to take over the reins of Italian banking – a family seemingly destined for greatness. In 1360, a man named Giovanni di Bicci de Medici was born. He grew up to be a merchant and, along with two of his sons, Cosimo the Elder and Lorenzo the Elder, created not only a powerful banking and mercantile dynasty, but a multi-generational political power as well. They became *the* dominant financial force in Europe. They intermarried with the royal families of the continent, and two Medici women, Marie and Catherine, became queens of France, fathering French kings as well. Meanwhile, two Medici sons, Giulio and Giovanni, became the Popes Clement VIII and Leo X, respectively. Numerous Medicis held other posts of importance in the Church and in government.

More important, perhaps, is that the Medicis quite purposefully used their influential positions to change the world for the better, and forever. They patronized the arts and letters, science and mathematics. They paid for the establishment of schools, churches, and hospitals. Because of their financial backing, the enlightened ideas of the Renaissance took hold with artists like Michelangelo and Botticelli, writers like Dante, and scientists like Galileo. Learning began to flourish once more, and the strangle-hold that the Catholic Church had held on learning began to lift, as artists now felt more free to compose human-centered rather than purely God-centered works, even in scenes depicting religious events. Christ and the Holy Family were now portrayed as more human, more real.

Indeed, most of our modern visual conceptions of the people, supernatural beings, and events described in the Bible are based on the art of the Medici-era Renaissance. So too is much of our Christian mythology. The Medici Popes used the power they held to modernize and liberalize the Church in a radical way. Certain ideas, such as the existence of Purgatory, were even appropriated in whole from the works of Dante. As a result of the Medicis' patronage of authors from Tuscany (their ancestral home and center of power), the Tuscan dialect of Latin became the predominant language of the Italian peninsula, and later developed into modern Italian.

In addition, their patronage of the study of philosophy and the sciences was equally influential. Although it would be many years before their views were widely accepted, thinkers like Galileo, whom the Medicis supported, were questioning the official Church version of the structure of the universe, in which, it was believed, the Sun and all other heavenly luminaries revolved around the Earth, the supposed center of God's creation. These new scientists and philosophers suspected that there was a whole new universe out there to be explored beyond this Earth, just as there was quite a bit of Earth yet left to be explored. These years were also the age of exploration, in which European royals (no doubt using money loaned to them by Medici bankers) paid daring navigators (descended from Templar families) to search for a new sea route to India, inadvertently (they say) proving radical new theories about the shape, size, and contents of planet Earth.

Authors Michael Baigent and Richard Leigh, in their book *Holy Blood, Holy Grail*, succinctly described the monumental nature of, in particular, Cosimo de Medici's contributions to society:

In 1439 ... Cosimo de Medici began sending his agents all over the world in quest of ancient manuscripts. Then, in 1444, Cosimo founded Europe's first public library, the Library of San Marco, and thus began to challenge the Church's long monopoly of learning. At Cosimo's express commission, the corpus of Platonic, Pythagorean, Gnostic, and hermetic thought found its way into translation for the first time and became readily accessible. Cosimo also instructed the University of Florence to begin teaching Greek for the first time in Europe for some seven hundred years. And he undertook to create an academy of Pythagorean and Platonic studies. Cosimo's academy quickly generated a multitude of similar institutions throughout the Italian peninsula, which became bastions of Western esoteric tradition.

One of the major developments to take place in Europe, starting from the time of the Templars and continuing on through the Medici years, was the widespread use of mathematics, not just by scholars or intellectuals, but by normal, everyday people for practical purposes. The revolution began with the introduction of Arabic, rather than Roman, numerals. It is the new Arabic numbers that we use now. (They had actually been adapted by the Arabs from an Indian system, although some scholars say that they are ultimately Chaldean in origin.) Roman numerals were notoriously difficult to calculate with, necessitating an abacus, jetton, and/or exchequer board. The existence of Arabic numerals was known in some circles, but had been frowned upon, for during the era of the Crusades, nobody wanted to touch the accursed symbols of the infidels. But the Italian merchants were already dealing with Arabs, and were in need of a more effective way of calculating their finances. Practicality won the day.

A watershed event was the publication of *Liber Abaci* by Leonardo Fibonacci, famous also for the discovery of the so-called "Fibonacci sequence", also called the "golden mean numbers", or the "Phi ratio". This was the book that really introduced Arabic numerals to the West. Notably, it occurred during the height of the Knights Templar's banking operations, which undoubtedly helped to spread the use of these numbers. Overnight, merchants discovered that there was a way of calculating numbers that was conceptually simple, and that could be done on a sheet of paper rather than using some cumbersome contraption. This new system was not immediately accepted. In fact, many colleges in Europe continued to teach Roman numerals exclusively until the 1600s. But in the meantime, the merchants made use of it. They were even responsible for the development of the "plus" (+) and "minus" (-) signs, which they used to mark shipments of goods that were overweight or underweight.

During the Medici years, many great strides were made in Italy in the field of mathematics. An anonymous text book from 1478 called *Treviso Arithmetic*, tailor-made for merchants, taught them how to multiply and divide. Nicolas Chuquet's 1484 *Triparty en la science des nombres* introduced the idea of separating numerals into groups of three, as we do now with commas (for example: 100,000), to make them easier to read. He also introduced words like "million" and "billion", to replace phrases like "a hundred hundred thousand." Luca Pacioli's 1487 treatise *Summa de aritmetica geometria proportioni et proportionalita* introduced double-entry book-keeping.

There were more ideas from the Arab East that got introduced into the West at this time. Algebra was developed in the ninth century by a man named Muhammad ibn-Musa al-Khwarizmi, but the word "algebra" entered European languages after having been lifted during the Renaissance from the title of his book: *Hisab al-Jabr w-al-Muqabalah* (*The Science of Restoration and Reduction*). Al-Khwarizmi also introduced the idea of decimals rather than fractions, and the term used in Europe at the time for them, "algorism" (a corruption of his name, Al-Khwarizmi), eventually became a more generalized term in mathematics. Mr. Al-Khwarizmi's ideas were actually introduced to the West by a Jewish scholar named Immanuel ben Jacob Bonfils of Tarascon in the year 1350.

It was only 250-300 years later, when the universities of Europe began to teach the new mathematics system, that people really began to understand the philosophical implications of mathematical principles. Math made philosophers realize many irrefutable truths, and taught them to look for truths that were quantifiable and unchanging, like mathematical axioms, rather than basing one's "facts" on faith in religious dogma. This paved the way for the revolutionary scientific discoveries of men like Rene Descartes and Sir Isaac Newton.

Thus developed the philosophy of the Enlightenment era, which held that the universe was rational, and could be understood using rational means. These ideas were promoted by the influential men involved in the newly-developing phenomenon of speculative Freemasonry, who also promoted the idea of a representative government, separated from the Church, so that no Pope, and no Pope's royal lackey, could ever again squelch scientific progress. The need for this form of government led to the colonization of America by Sir Francis Bacon's Virginia Company, with the aim of turning this new country into the ultimate philosophic empire, where learning and discovery could thrive without interference and indeed, would be encouraged.

All of these amazing changes occurred in European society from the end of the Dark Ages, signaled by the accomplishments of the Knights Templar, through the Italian merchant and banking years (which ended with the collapse of the Medici bank in 1494, following the French invasion of Florence by King Charles VIII, and the expulsion of the Medicis from the city), on through the Enlightenment era. In this series of widely diverse events, separated by space and time, we can detect a certain continuity.

To understand what I mean, let us go back to the year 324, when Constantinople was founded.

Chapter Eight:
The Empire in the East
and the Church of the Holy Wisdom

When the newly-converted Christian emperor of Rome began raising funds to found his new capitol in the East, Constantine made a point of using gold coins minted from the melted down idols of Roman pagan temples to pay for the construction. It was an "f- you" not only to the gods of Rome, but to Rome itself, for in founding Constantinople, the emperor was establishing a "New Rome." But he really intended for it to be the recreation of another ancient city - Jerusalem.

Already his mother, Helena, had been converted to Christianity along with him, and had become so devout that she made a pilgrimage to Jerusalem in search of the grave of Christ. A lucky woman, that Helena. She just happened not only to discover Jesus' tomb, but remnants of the True Cross, the Crown of Thorns, and numerous other holy relics. She had churches erected on the spots where she found these items. Constantine, too, erected churches, mainly the first St. Peter's Basilica in Rome, and the first "Hagia Sophia" (the "Church of the Holy Wisdom") in Constantinople.

The change of the capital of the Roman Empire from Rome to Constantinople had major effects on the development of the Catholic Church. Constantine's successor, Theodosius I, held an ecumenical council in 381 in which it was declared that the Bishop of Constantinople would be second in Christendom only to the bishop of Rome. Theodosius officially banned pagan cults, and began closing any pagan temples that remained. But although the church in Rome and the church in Constantinople had started out as the same church, East and West began to divide theologically and culturally, until they were eventually two separate churches, and two separate empires: the one waning, the other rising. The Byzantine Empire lasted from 324 to 1453, and at its height included Northern Italy, Macedonia, Southern Spain, Turkey, Bulgaria, North Africa, and parts of Egypt. As the Empire grew, the Byzantines reverted back entirely to the Greek language, and in many ways continued the Greek traditions by fostering within their empire a cultural love of Greek philosophy, art, and literature.

It was during the rule of Byzantine Emperor Justinian I that an unfortunate incident occurred involving Constantine's Hagia Sophia. In 532, a riot broke out in the sports stadium known as the Hippodrome, the conflict being between fans of the blue chariot team and the red chariot team. It was the ancient equivalent of a soccer hooligan brawl. The melee spread throughout the city, and before long the Hagia Sophia had been completely trashed. Justinian had all those still rioting in the Hippodrome massacred, and that put an end to the riot. Afterwards he had the church rebuilt more magnificently than ever before. It immediately became the most renowned building in Christendom, and remained so until St. Peter's Basilica was rebuilt to extravagance during the Medici years. As one author, Benita Goldman of Eastern Michigan University put it in her essay, *Byzantium and Her Arts*:

Hagia Sophia was rebuilt on a daring scale.....the dome was so large, the interior so spacious, that visitors said the dome itself appeared to be resting on light, or suspended from heaven by a golden chain. The example of Hagia Sophia was so profound that, as the Byzantine Empire expanded and contracted, not one corner of it did not prefer a church with a central dome. The Eastern Orthodox structures of Russia, Greece and Bulgaria all pay homage to the church of Holy Wisdom. Even the humblest Eastern Orthodox structure could hardly be called complete without a dome. Just as with the Greek culture and the Romans who revered it (the captors were held by their captives in thrall), the later inhabitants of Constantinople, the Ottoman Turks, even devised their Imperial Mosques after the example of Hagia Sophia.

To finish off his creation, Justinian took precious, expensive decorations from older temples all over the empire, and used them for Hagia Sophia instead. When he was done, he was said to have exclaimed: "Solomon, I have outdone you", a reference to the opulent temple which King Solomon had built in Jerusalem to house the Ark of the Covenant, equally encrusted with gold and jewels.

Byzantium went through a great deal of turmoil throughout the history of its empire, expanding and contracting in size as it continually fought off invasion from barbarian and Muslim hordes. Their church (now the Eastern Orthodox Church) was even influenced somewhat by Islam, in that they began to take on the ideology of iconoclasm. Islam shunned the depiction of any living form in nature as idolatry, and would allow only abstract, geometric art forms. In contrast, Christianity, both the Roman and the Eastern Orthodox varieties, made great use of art and architecture depicting Christ, the Holy Family, and religious themes. They did not shy away from using these depictions in their rituals, either. The Eastern Orthodox Church even made use of what they called "icons", by which they specifically meant portraits of saints which one would pray to, asking the saint to intercede on one's behalf, and pass the prayer on to

Jesus. Author Benita Goldman explains in further detail the role these items play in church ritual:

The Iconostasis or 'Icon Wall' in a Byzantine or Eastern Orthodox Church is a screen separating the faithful from the divine and mysterious rituals of the Holy Sacrament. Unlike the Catholic Church, this ritual takes place behind a wall or screen, rather than at the altar in front of the congregation. Commonly, the Iconostasis is painted with the Deesis (literally, the 'entreaty'). This is an arrangement of the following elements: Christ enthroned centrally, flanked by St. John the Baptist and the Virgin Mary (the Theotokos.) Both St. John and Mary are most frequently depicted making prayerful entreaties to the enthroned Christ...

In Russia, most homes had an 'icon corner' where the icon was placed. Icons were believed to have a miraculous power of protection over the home and its occupants. Some icons, such as the famous Virgin of Vladimir, were thought to protect the city. Often, these famous icons were embellished with covers in precious metal and gems. The Virgin of Vladimir was revered enough to have several such covers, embellished through the years in silver and gold...

Similar practices existed, and still exist, in the Catholic Church, which also encourages its members to pray to statues and portraits of Jesus, the Holy family, and other saints. So when the Orthodox Church went through two waves of Iconoclasm, in which the use of images was prohibited, it further drove a wedge between them and the Catholic Church. This is why in the year 800, Pope Leo II personally crowned a new Emperor of the Western Romans, Charlemagne, creating the Holy Roman Empire which was to last in Europe for 1000 years, subverting the power that Empress Irene of Constantinople believed she still held in the West.

To do this, the Pope asserted a document called "the Donation of Constantine", that he claimed had been drafted and signed by the Thirteenth Apostle himself, in which Constantine supposedly "donated" his imperial power to Church, giving the Pope the power to crown kings. Constantine, of course, would never have signed such a thing, and the document is now universally regarded by scholars as a fraud. But it remained the basis of the Holy Roman Empire for the rest of its duration, although of course it went totally unrecognized by the now completely separate Eastern Church and Empire. The Western ruler became known as the "Imperator Romanorum" ("Emperor of the Romans"), and the Eastern ruler became known as the "Imperator Graecorum" ("Emperor of the Greeks"). The schism between the churches was finalized in 1054.

The Crusades of the Holy Roman Empire to capture Jerusalem would have an inadvertently negative effect on Constantinople. In the year 1096 the First Crusade traveled through the city en route to the holy land. The Roman Catholic soldiers were feeling spiteful towards their Eastern Orthodox rivals, so they sacked the city, and other nearby domains, as they passed through. The same thing happened in 1204 during the Fourth Crusade, only this time they not only pillaged it: they actually set up their own "Latin Kingdom" in the city. The Eastern Orthodox Greeks managed to take the city back in 1261, but it didn't last too much longer. However the great Constantinople fell at last not to fellow Christians, but to the Muslim Ottoman Turks. Benita Goldman describes the dramatic fall of the empire on May 29, 1453:

The final day ... came ... at the hands of the Ottoman Sultan, Mehmet the Conqueror. The great iron chain, bits of which can be seen today in the Istanbul Archaeological Museum, was forged by the Byzantines to protect the water routes that led to the city. The Byzantines stretched their chain across the water and fortified the walls. The great Theodosian walls were manned with marksmen, but Constantinople in these last days was alone. She had lost her territories, and when she called for help none responded to the call. The last Byzantine Emperor, named Constantine Paleologus, went from bastion to bastion along the walls, cheering the men and urging them to strength. At midnight May 28, the faithful said their last prayers in Hagia Sophia. The Turks, led by Sultan Mehmet II, portaged their boats over land, bypassing the great chain of the Byzantines. With a 26 foot canon, the Turks were able to pierce the walls of the city. The Turks then entered Constantinople. They erected a crescent moon over Hagia Sophia, replacing the cross over the dome. On a white charger, Mehmet the Conqueror entered Hagia Sophia and declared it a mosque. That was the end of the Byzantine Empire, although not of its influence nor its legacy to the world.

As we all know from the popular They Might Be Giants tune, if nothing else, the city once known as "Constantinople" is now called "Istanbul."

Chapter Nine:
The Head of Prophecy and the Aegis of the Goat

Let us return now to the concept of the "Baphomet", the idol which the Knights Templar were found guilty of worshipping, purportedly because it "caused the land to germinate", and "made them rich." These facts, coupled with the fact that the idol was often depicted as a goat with male and female sexual organs, might cause one to think that the Templars had somehow stumbled upon and absorbed the tenets of the cult of the she-goat Amalthea. This is the creature who purportedly nursed Zeus while he was a babe in exile on the island of Crete, hiding from his father Kronos, who wished to kill him. Her name means "tender", specifically referring to that definition of tender as "a person who attends to or takes charge of someone or some thing" (*Webster's Dictionary*), not the financial term. Having little thanks for the favors of Amalthea, Zeus had her slaughtered as soon as he was fully grown, and fashioned from her skin an impenetrable shield called the "Aegis." The word "aegis" or "aigis" literally means "goat-skin."

Zeus would shake this shield (emblazoned with the image of the severed head of Gorgon) in the air in order to create thunder, and thus he earned the epithet "Aigiokhos", meaning "wielder of the goat-skin." Zeus used this shield when he went to battle against the Titans. He also used the "cornucopia" or "horn of plenty", which he made from one of Amalthea's horns: a magical object that contained an inexhaustible supply of fruits and flowers. After he had killed her and used all of her parts that he wanted, Zeus placed Amalthea amongst the stars, where she became the constellation of Capricorn. The figure of Capricorn then came to be thought of as a "sea-goat", since she resided in the "celestial sea" of Heaven.

So Amalthea was venerated by some cults in much the same way that the vegetation deity known as the "Green Man" was in Celtic culture: as a representative of nature, of fecundity, plenteousness, and thus, by extension, wealth. Baphomet was so literally associated with money by the Templars that they kept small statuettes of him in their money coffers. But the Baphomet is reported to have done more for the Templars besides just make them rich. He is also said to have made them "wise." In fact, it has been shown that Baphomet's name literally means "wisdom."

I explained previously that the Templars made use of cryptograms, or ciphers, in the checking system that they invented. One of the ciphers that they used most often was a simple one called "Atbash", in which the first letter of the alphabet is replaced with the last letter of the alphabet, then the second replaced with the second-to-last, etc. It has been discovered that if the letters of "Baphomet" are converted into Aramaic (a late Hebrew-Greek blend used in the New Testament), and then run through the Atbash cipher, you get the word "sophia", which means "wisdom." "Sophia" was indeed the name used for the goddess of wisdom, who was often revered in Gnostic cults in New Testament times. It was believed in these cults that one could unite spiritually with Sophia by performing certain rites and meditations, and thus obtain "gnosis", or divine knowledge. In addition to the message rendered from the Atbash cipher, according to the 1865 tome *Worship of the Generative Powers*, by Thomas Right, Baphomet was sometimes referred to simply as "Mete" by Templars, a word which in itself means "wisdom" (as I shall explain in greater detail later on).

Gnosticism was widely practiced in the Roman Empire during Christ's time. One man widely believed to have been a Gnostic was John the Baptist, the prophet of the New Testament who announced the coming of Christ. John was, after his death, himself revered by a number of Gnostic cults. There were even, by medieval times, numerous underground "Christian" sects called "Johannites", who believes that John was the true Messiah. Johannite cults even exist today in the form of semi-Islamic Gnostic sects found in Iraq. It has been charged that that Templars followed this doctrine, and indeed, he was their patron saint, as he is now for Freemasonry. More importantly, perhaps, he is known to have been beheaded at the Temple Mount in Jerusalem, and his head, or skull, has become a central Christian icon. This brings into focus the claim of occultist Aleister Crowley that the name "Baphomet", by itself, without running it through any ciphers, means "Baptist of Wisdom." Given what we know of John, this could easily have been a title for the prophet himself.

So can John's head be the skull that the Templars are said to have not only worshipped, but talked to? Specifically it is said to have "prophesied" for them. In the Gnostic text *The Apocryphon of St James*, John's severed head is referred to as "the head of prophecy." It says:

Then I questioned him: 'Lord how may we prophesy to those who ask us to prophesy to them? For there are many who ask us and who look to us to hear an oracle from us.'
The Lord answered and said: 'Do you not know that the head of prophecy was cut off with John?'

And I said: 'Lord, it is not possible to remove the head of prophecy, is it?'

The Lord said to me: 'When you come to know what 'head' is, and that prophecy issues from the head, then understand what is the meaning of 'Its head was removed.' I first spoke with you in parables, and you did not understand. Now, in turn, I speak with you openly, and you do not perceive.'

Moreover, the use of a severed head or skull for divination was a common practice throughout the ancient East and even, though secretly, in Judah and Israel during Old Testament times. Such devices were called "teraphim", as defined by the online Jewish Encyclopedia:

...the teraphim were made of the head of a man, a first-born which, after the man had been slain, was shaved and then salted and spiced. After a gold plate on which magic words were engraved had been placed under the tongue, the mummified head was mounted on the wall... lighted candles were placed round it; the people then prostrated themselves before it, and it spoke to them.

Likewise, famous mystic H.P. Blavatsky wrote an article alleging that the practice continued on into Renaissance Europe. The article is called "Animated Statues", written for her magazine, *The Theosophist*. In it she wrote:

[Thesaurist] Ugolino puts in the mouth of the sage Gamaliel, St. Paul's master (or guru), the following words, which he quotes, he says, from his Capito, *chap. xxxvi: 'They (the possessors of such necromantic teraphim) killed a new-born baby, cut off its head, and placed under its tongue, salted and oiled, a little gold lamina in which the name of an evil spirit was perforated; then, after suspending that head on the wall of their chamber, they lighted lamps before it, and prostrate on the ground they conversed with it.'...*

In the Middle Ages... several Roman Catholic priests are known to have resorted to [this practice]; among others the apostate Jacobin priest in the service of Queen Catherine of Medici, that faithful daughter of the Church of Rome and the author of the St. Bartholomew Massacre. The story is given by [Jean] Bodin, in his famous work on Sorcery, Le Demonomanie, ou Traité des Sorciers *(Paris, 1587); and it is quoted in* Isis Unveiled *(Vol. ii, p. 56). Pope Sylvester II was publicly accused by*

Cardinal Benno of sorcery, on account of his Brazen Oracular Head.'

This is exactly what many scholars believe Baphomet was for the Templars: a teraph made from the head or skull of John the Baptist. It is interesting, then, that Ms. Blavatsky tied the Medici family to the use of teraphim, for reasons that will become clear later on in this book. The same connection was made by Manly P. Hall, who wrote in his essay "Ceremonial Magick and Sorcery, An Holy Excerpt from his Greate Alchymeckal Worke of 1928" (from *The Secret Teachings of All Ages: An Encyclopaedic Outline of Masonic, Hermetic, Qabbalistic and Rosicrucian Symbolical Philosophy*) the following:

The little red daemon of Napoleon Bonaparte and the infamous oracular heads of de Medici are examples of the disastrous results of permitting elemental beings to dictate the course of human procedure.

So how would the Templars have gotten a hold of the skull of John the Baptist? Well, during their formative years, the Templars were stationed at the Al-Aqsa Mosque in Jerusalem, right there on the mountain itself. It was the fact that they were formed there, at the site of what was once the great Jewish temple, which gave the Order its name, "the Poor Knights of Christ of the Temple of Solomon."

Since the Knights Templar are known to have explored the secret caves beneath the Temple Mount (looking for the Ark of the Covenant, some say), it is quite possible that they discovered the head of John while down there. It is also possible that they picked it up from Constantinople while they were passing through to Jerusalem for the First Crusade. While most of the soldiers were busy with more ordinary raping and pillaging, the Templars could have been on a systematic hunt for any religious relics that might have been housed there.

There were of course, many of them there. For a while this had been the center of Christendom, and is the most likely place for Constantine to have housed some of the relics found by his mother, Helena, in her search through the Holy Land. Of course, most of the relics she found are accounted for, and were venerated in churches that she had erected in Jerusalem, and also in Rome. But some ended up in Constantinople, and I think that is the likely landing place for any relics deemed too precious to put on public display. I can even see Constantine and Helena plotting to put fake relics on display in the various churches, and hiding the real ones in the original Hagia Sophia.

There are indeed stories of the skull of John the Baptist having ended up there. The most widely-accepted claimant to the title has long been the skull on display in Antioch. But there was another claimant that was put on display in Constantinople and was venerated by the royalty of Aquitaine, Gaul, Italy, and Spain, who all made a pilgrimage to the Byzantine capital to celebrate its translation there by Emperor Theodosius. One of the interesting things about this skull is that it was, according to contemporary chronicler Ademar of Chabannes, "enclosed in a stone reliquary formed in the shape of a pyramid." When it was installed in its new home, fantastic powers were ascribed to the relic:

During that same period, the relics of St. Eparchius were brought in procession to John the Baptist. The staff of office of that same confessor was also brought along; this pastoral staff was curved at its head. As long as these relics were there with the head of John the Baptist, a fiery baculus, curved at its top in a manner similar to that of Eparchius, shone forth in the night sky until dawn over the relics. Other miracles in curing the sick were performed by Eparchius, before his relics were brought home in happiness. The canons of Saint-Pierre of Angoulême also brought their relics on procession [to Angèly]. When those who were carrying the relics had to roll up their sacred tunics and wade through a deep river, they did not feel the water, but walked as through a desert, moreover no sign of water appeared on them, on their clothing, or on their sandals. Meanwhile, after the head of St. John had been adequately exhibited to the populace, it was returned on orders of Duke William to the pyramid in which it had originally been housed, in the interior of which it was suspended in its new reliquary by silver chains. The stone pyramid was covered with wooden panels which were lined with silver, taken from the large gift of silver which King Sanchio of Navarre had brought to the blessed herald. The relics continued to be arranged thus long after these events occurred.

Another description of these events, from *The Nicene & Post-Nicene Fathers Of The Christian Church, Second Series, Volume II*, edited by Philip Schaff, was even more bizarre:

About this time the head of John the Baptist, which Herodias had asked of Herod the tetrarch, was removed to Constantinople. It is said that it was discovered by some monks of the Macedonian heresy, who originally dwelt at Constantinople, and afterwards fixed their abode in Cilicia. Mardonius, the first eunuch of the palace, made known this discovery at court, during the preceding reign; and Valens commanded that the relic should be removed to Constantinople.

The officers appointed to carry it thither, placed it in a public chariot, and proceeded with it as far as Pantichium, a district in the territory of Chalcedon. Here the mules of the chariot suddenly stopped; and neither the application of the lash, nor the threats of the hostlers, could induce them to advance further. So extraordinary an event was considered by all, and even by the emperor himself, to be of God; and the holy head was therefore deposited at Cosilaos, a village in the neighborhood, which belonged to Mardonius. Soon after, the Emperor Theodosius, impelled by an impulse from God, or from the prophet, repaired to the village.

He determined upon removing the remains of the Baptist, and it is said met with no opposition, except from a holy virgin, Matrona, who had been the servant and guardian of the relic. He laid aside all authority and force, and after many entreaties, extorted a reluctant consent from her to remove the head; for she bore in mind what had occurred at the period when Valens commanded its removal. The emperor placed it, with the box in which it was encased, in his purple robe, and conveyed it to a place called Hebdomos, in the suburbs of Constantinople, where he erected a spacious and magnificent temple.

I think the insertion of the character of "Matrona" is interesting, and I feel that she represents here the wisdom goddess Sophia, the female personification of Baphomet.

Besides the skull of John itself, there is another candidate for the Baphomet which is also an artifact that the Templars may have obtained from Constantinople. It was called "the Mandylion." This object's official story is described in full and adequately by the website printeryhouse.org, which sells reproductions of Greek Orthodox Christian icons:

This image is considered to be the oldest known icon and also the oldest known portrait of Jesus. According to ancient legend, King Abgar of Edessa, (now Urfa in Turkey), was a leper. He sent his archivist named Hannan (or Ananias) to Galilee with a letter to Jesus, beseeching Him to come to Edessa and heal him. Hannan was a painter and had orders to make a portrait of the Lord in case he refused to come. Hannan came upon Jesus in the midst of a large crowd. He tried to make a portrait but could not. Seeing Hannan's need, Jesus asked for some water, washed himself, and wiping His face on a linen cloth, imprinted it with his features. When Abgar beheld the cloth, his leprosy was cured, although his scars remained. After Pentecost, the apostle Thaddeus, one of the seventy, went to Edessa and completed Abgar's cure and conversion to Christianity.

The image of Christ on the linen cloth was preserved for centuries in Edessa as the city's most sacred treasure. The legend and the image are referred to by many ancient writers, such as Eusebius of Caesarea (325 AD), and Evagrius (590 AD). In 944, the Byzantines captured the image from Edessa, which was under Moslem rule, and brought it with great ceremony to Constantinople. The event is still celebrated in the Orthodox liturgical calendar on August 16. It remained there until the sack of that city by the crusaders in 1204, when it disappeared. But by that time, innumerable icons had been made, preserving the sacred image to this day.

The image has been referred to in many ways over the centuries. In Greek, it is called the 'Achieropoietos,' meaning 'not made by human hands,' in keeping with its miraculous origin. It has also been called the Mandylion, literally 'little handkerchief.' This word having an Arabic root, was used in Byzantium only to describe this image. In iconography, there are two variants; a version with Christ's hair and beard curly and flowing, and this version with beard wet and forked.

There are similarities between this object and descriptions of the object worshipped by the Templars. The most obvious is that it shows the disembodied head of a bearded man, as the head of Baphomet is said to have been. Also, if the Mandylion were the mystically-created imprint of a man's face, like the Shroud of Turin supposedly is of Christ's body, it might look as the Shroud does, like a photo negative, and thus, somewhat skull-like. If this is indeed what Baphomet was, one can see how it could have been reported, by knights who were exposed to it, as both a bearded head, and a skull. They might have thought it looked a little bit "goaty" as well.

But another important similarity between Baphomet and the Mandylion is its possible use for divination. The Mandylion was used by the Byzantine Church as an "icon", and copies of it are still used as such in the Greek Orthodox Church today. You will recall that with these icons, people believe that they can directly contact the saint or divine being depicted on them. Is it not possible that with an icon such as the Mandylion, which was also a holy relic, an imprint of the Savior's own face, some people believed that it could talk *back* to them as well? Or especially so, if the head that was actually depicted on the cloth was the "head of prophecy", that of John the Baptist?

In an article entitled "The Templars, The Shroud, the Veil and the Mandylion" on the website templarhistory.com, Chevalier John Ritchie (a member of the neo-templar group the Sovereign Military Order of the Temple of Jerusalem) suggests that the Mandylion did depict the head of John the Baptist, and that it was the same as the Baphomet of the Templars. He suggests that they obtained it during the sacking of Constantinople in 1204, during the Fourth Crusade, after which the Crusaders set up a "Latin Kingdom" in Constantinople. As he describes it:

The most likely possessors of the Mandylion would appear to be the Order of the Knights Templar. They were the first troops into Constantinople in 1204, they knew of the imperial collection, and were in fact the body guard to Count Baldwin of Flanders [the newly-crowned Latin King in Constantinople], so it would have been very easy for them to obtain the Mandylion and other relics during the sacking.

Ritchie also suggests that it was not unusual for Templar depictions of Baphomet to be flat, wall-mounted portraits rather than standing idols:

...every Templar Preceptory had a copy of this 'head', and one of these came to light in England in 1951, during the demolition of an outhouse at Templecombe Somerset, the site of a long vanished Templar preceptory. This was a curious panel painting covered with dust but clearly depicting a bearded male head of the type referred to in the confessions forced from the Knights Templar under... Today this Templecombe panel hangs in the church of St. Mary. Templecombe, its resemblance to the face on the Mandylion is unmistakable.

Chapter Ten:
A Contract With Baphomet

But how could possessing an item such as the Mandylion, or a mummified severed head, make the Templars rich? Well, let us just suspend disbelief for a moment and swallow the Templars' own beliefs. Obviously they believed that Baphomet could talk to them, and that Baphomet possessed "divine wisdom." So right off the bat, with that belief as our basis, it is possible to contend that Baphomet taught the Templars all forms of knowledge, including the mysteries of money and wealth. It is evident that the Templars did come into possession of great sources of wisdom, which enabled them to be involved in breath-through accomplishments of art, science and medicine during their time. And the ideas they applied to create their international banking system were sheer genius.

But more than that, it is clear that the Templars afforded the image of Baphomet itself a certain ceremonial reverence, accrediting it with a certain talismanic power, which demonstrates that they believed their devotion to it, and their sacrifices to it, would gain them wealth in return. This is a very ancient concept, and one which I will get into in greater detail later on. It is the belief that one can contact a deity through divination and negotiate a contract with it, in which one agrees to perform certain services for the deity, in exchange for blessings in return.

A deity whose symbolism was associated with the very idea of a divine contract was the Persian god Mithras. He was known as the "god of contracts", and the inventor of the legal system. People would invoke him as a witness when drawing up a contract of any sort between two parties, and it was believed that he would punish severely all those who broke their contracts. These deals would be sealed with a handshake which, according to mythology, was another invention of Mithras', first taught by him to mankind when he was inducting priests into his cult. In the rites of Mithras, the initiates were made to shake the hand of Mithras (usually played in the ritual by another cult member) as a seal of a pact between the inductee and his new teacher, Mithras, referred to in the ritual by the nickname "the Friend." Many aspects of this ritual were absorbed into the rites of Freemasonry.

The name "Mithras" is related to words in all ancient languages that mean 'to measure." These root words have resulted in modern terms like "metric", "method", "medicine", and "mathematics." This is because Mithras was also known for having taught basic math, science, and medicine to mankind in ancient times. The root word "mitr" has been said to actually communicate the more generalized concept of "knowledge" or "wisdom." Indeed, according to several modern occult scholars, including author Nicholas de Vere (*The Dragon Legacy, USA, 2004*), the name "Baphomet" means "Father Mithras" or "Father of Wisdom."

Mithras was a solar deity, and the cult of Sol Invictus in Rome, followed by Emperor Constantine even after his conversion to Christianity, was very much an offshoot of the cult of Mithras. It is noteworthy that the "sign" which he saw in his divine vision, when he was told by God "In this sign you will conquer", was not the Christian cross, or even the equilateral cross later used by the Templars, but actually the "Chi Rho" symbol, made from the first two letters of Christ's name in Greek. Or at least, that is what Christians today say its meaning and origin is. According to most scholars it actually has a pre-Christian origin, and was used by the ancient cult of Sol Invictus. But the fact remains that after his vision, Constantine had the symbol inscribed on the shields of his soldiers, who then went charging into battle against his rival for the throne. His army was victorious. He became the emperor, converted to Christianity, and moved the capitol of his empire to a new city which he had built – Constantinople.

It seems to me that the Chi Rho symbol, which looks like a modern letter "P" on top of a modern letter "X", greatly resembles the skull and crossbones symbol of the Templars, the simple hieroglyph they used to represent Baphomet. It was also a symbol of Mithras. In a segment about the Chi Rho in the classic Masonic textbook, *Morals and Dogma*, Albert Pike wrote that:

The Cross, X, was the sign of the Creative Wisdom or Logos, the Son of God... Mithras signed his soldiers on the forehead with a Cross.

So let us say for the sake of argument that the Baphomet was a talisman of some sort that, among other things bestowed upon its possessor 'wisdom" and "riches" – or more specifically, the power to both *gain* and *create* wealth. Let us say that Constantine somehow came into possession of it, perhaps when his mother Helena was in Jerusalem digging around for holy relics. His religious vision may have foreshadowed this discovery, or even led him and his mother to it. Or it might have just been a story made up after the fact. It is also possible that it was already there in Rome in some hidden vault known only to the emperor, and Constantine only learned of it after he ascended to the throne. The Romans, of course, had taken over the land of Judah, and had sacked Jerusalem, carrying off all of the treasures of the Temple that they found. If this was the case, Helena's treasure hunt in Jerusalem could have been simply to find more artifacts.

At any rate, as my hypothesis goes, Constantine used the power of this talisman to create his new empire in Constantinople. In this proposed version of events, he would have formed a "divine contract" with the deity represented by the talisman, just as the Templars would have later done with Baphomet. He created a temple to house this relic, the "Hagia Sophia", or "Church of the Holy Wisdom" – or in other words, the Church of Baphomet. Constantine then sacrificed to this idol all of the wealth from the temples of Rome's pagan gods. That is, he sacrificed everything dedicated to the old religion, the old "divine contracts", and put them in the service of his new religion, his new "divine contract" with Baphomet. In exchange, Byzantium became the global center of wisdom and learning, and the most beautiful, most wealthy city in the whole world. It was an empire that lasted over 1100 years. It was only when Constantinople fell to the Turks in 1452 that the European Renaissance is said to have fully kicked into high gear, when all of the Jewish and Greek Orthodox scholars who had been living there fled the Muslim terror and sought relative safety in Europe.

So let us then say that the Templars took control of this artifact in turn. This could have happened in their first pass through the city in 1090, when they and other crusaders sacked it on their way to the First Crusades. It was only after this – after capturing Jerusalem and becoming stationed on the Temple Mount – that they formally organized themselves into an order. Then they started digging for buried treasure there, just as Constantine's mother had done after (in my proposed scenario) Constantine came into the possession of Baphomet. Perhaps Baphomet operates better as a talisman and divination device when it is used in conjunction with other holy relics. Perhaps that explains why the Templars were eager to get the Mandylion, which could have been a copy of the Baphomet head, rather than the original.

After coming to possess the Baphomet, I think the Knights formed a pact with the deity connected to it, and began to structure their order into an international system for advancing learning and science, and for creating wealth – exactly as Constantine had done by creating the Byzantine Empire. Their wealth and membership expanded exponentially after they created a formal constitution for their Order, which must have been an extension of their pact with Baphomet. As Michael Baigent and Richard

Leigh describe in their book *The Temple and the Lodge*:

Until 1128... the Templars were said to have consisted only of nine knights... Then, at The Council of Troyes, conducted under the auspices of Saint Bernard, the Templars were given a monastic rule, the equivalent, so to speak, of a constitution, and were thereby formally established...

From 1128 on, the Order expanded at an extraordinary pace, receiving not just a massive influx of recruits, but also immense donations of both money and property. Within a year, they owned lands in France, England, Scotland, Spain, and Portugal. Within a decade, their possessions would extend to Italy, Austria, Germany, Hungary, and Constantinople. In 1131, the king of Aragon bequeathed to them a third of his domains. By the mid-twelfth century, the Temple had already begun to establish itself as the single most wealthy and powerful institution in Christendom, with the sole exception of the Papacy.

If the Templars did possess this "Baphomet", capable of bestowing wisdom and, more importantly, wealth, this may explain what both King Philippe IV and Pope Clement V were itching to take from the Templars when they engineered their arrest, even if they did not fully understand what it was they were looking for. It is said that Philippe's seneschals searched frantically all throughout the Templar properties in France, seeking their fabled "treasure", for he knew they were rich. But he did not really understand that their wealth was created by banking, and was spread throughout their domains, invested in various money-making enterprises. Only a fraction of it actually existed in reserve as physical currency. Alan Butler and Stephen Dafoe described the situation in their book *The Warriors and the Bankers: A History of the Knights Templar from 1307 to the Present*:

Templar treasuries there may have been, and their accumulated values must have been incredible, but it would have been economic and political suicide to keep one vast depository. It should also be mentioned that much of the Templars' wealth was constantly moving about, and was being used to make more money, thickening out the services on offer and expanding the business empire. The Templars owned vast areas of land in almost every Western European country, the accumulated revenues of which went to finance bigger and better ventures – all run by a staff who were not paid in the general sense of the word, but whose efficiency was legendary. It is a fact of history that neither Philip IV, or anyone else, ever found the Templar treasure that was said to exist, though this may, in part, be due to the same sort of careful pre-planning that ensured the survival of the majority of Templar personnel. Just as surely as De Molay could take care of the brothers and servants of his order... so he must surely have ensured that movable wealth, in the form of treasure and objects, was spirited away to locations beyond the jurisdiction of the French Crown. Unfortunately, the Templars' greatest asset – farm land – could not be moved, and this form of treasure ultimately did fall to either the Knights Hospitaller, or, in many cases, to the monarchs of Europe... It is likely a great deal of their wealth passed to organizations which took their place, such as the Knights of Christ in Portugal...

After the Templars were disbanded, many of them were sentenced to penance in monasteries, and thus they ended up joining these other knightly orders, including the Knights of Christ, the Knights Hospitaller, and the Teutonic Knights. Despite the wishes of King Philippe to claim everything for himself, Pope Clement V stepped in and had most of the Templars' properties transferred to these other orders, especially the Knights Hospitaller.

It is the Hospitallers who I believe most likely inherited the Baphomet, or at least, the secrets of wealth creation which it had imparted to the Knights Templar. The Hospitallers were a rival order during the Templars' time, especially known, as the name implies, for setting up hospitals throughout Europe, which operated with what was, at the time, cutting-edge medical technology. Like the Templars, their patron saint was John the Baptist. Their full name was actually "the Knights Hospitaller of St. John", but it was later changed to just "the Knights of Saint John." They eventually changed their name again to the one we know them as today: the "Knights of Malta." In their book *The Messianic Legacy*, Michael Baigent, Richard Leigh, and Henry Lincoln described the origins of this group:

The Order of Saint John originated with a hospital dedicated to Saint John in Jerusalem and established around 1070, some thirty years before the First Crusade, by Italian merchants to minister to pilgrims... By 1126... the Knights of Saint John had begun to assume and increasingly military character which was soon to eclipse, though not altogether supplant, their Hospitaller services. In the years that followed, they came to comprise, along with the Templars and subsequently the Teutonic Knights, the major military and financial power in the Holy Land, and one of the major such powers in all Christendom. Like the Templars, they became immensely wealthy.

The Hospitallers began to increase their membership and take on a more military character in 1126, just two years before the Templars began their own first major expansion of manpower and landholdings. However, the true "heyday" of the Hospitallers seems to have come *after* the fall of the Templars in 1307. Just two years later, in 1309, they moved their headquarters to the island of Rhodes, which, according to *The Messianic Legacy*, they "governed as their private principality." After three sieges by the Turks, they moved to another island, Malta, in 1530. By the 1600s, the Order's significance had waned according to Baigent, et. al. They write:

By the seventeenth century, the knights still resident on Malta had been left behind by the tide of history, a staunch Catholic enclave still adhering to obsolete chivalric tenets while the rest of Europe moved into a new age of mercantilism and middle-class hegemony.

Nevertheless, they continued to operate in Malta until Napoleon invaded the island in 1798. They re-established themselves in Rome in 1834 and strangely, only then did they change their name to "Order of Malta", to distinguish themselves from other, Protestant, Orders of St. John that had cropped up since their initial inception.

Here in Rome, they settled into a role which they continue to this day. They act as an unofficial intelligence service for the Vatican. They also possess a "sovereignty" granted by the Church which operates in much the same way that the Knights Templar's similarly granted sovereignty once did, and although the Church no longer holds the sway it used to over the governments of the world, these states still recognize the sovereignty of the Knights of Malta. Baigent, et. al. describe in *The Messianic Legacy* the role that the Knights now play in international affairs:

In international law, the current status of the Knights of Malta is that of an independent sovereign principality. The Grand Master is recognized as a head of state, with a secular rank equivalent to a prince and an ecclesiastical rank equivalent to a cardinal. The Order maintains formal diplomatic relations with a number of countries, especially in Africa and Latin American, and in those countries its ministers enjoy standard diplomatic privileges. The upper grades of the Order are still fastidiously aristocratic. The highest Knights must be able to display a coat of arms dating back at least three hundred years, in unbroken succession from father to son.

The twentieth-century Order of Malta is, needless to say, ideally placed for intelligence work. Its network of membership is international and at the same time well-organized. Its hospital and medical services often place it strategically at points of crisis... Its membership extends from medical staff and ambulance drivers to important figures in politics, business and finance who have access to spheres that ordinary priests would not. In consequence, the Knights of Malta became closely associated with the Vatican's own intelligence department...

The book then goes on to describe how the Knights of Malta liaised for decades with the CIA and European intelligence organizations, as well as other Catholic and right-wing political groups during the latter half of the twentieth century. They worked together to fund and organize an anti-Communist united Europe movement (which has now succeeded in creating the European Union), as well as anti-Communist movements in Latin America. It is also known that many of these knights work for banks and financial institutions that handle the Vatican's accounts.

So could there be a relationship between the Italian merchant families that set up the Knights of St. John, and the Italian merchant families that came to dominate international finance during the post-Templar Renaissance era? Moreover, is not it likely that the secret contingent of Knights Templar, those who may have smuggled the Baphomet head to safety when the Templars were disbanded, also continued the Baphometic tradition of finance by sharing the secrets of wealth creation with these families? Like all chivalric knightly orders, both the Knights Templar and the Knights of St. John were strictly aristocratic organizations meant only for those of noble birth. Of course, all noble families were genetically connected one way or another through common ancestry because of the aristocratic tradition of marrying close to one's own gene pool. So a relationship between Templar and Hospitaller families, and thus, by extension, Italian merchant families, is implicit. It may be significant, then, that the Florentine florin, which became one of the two standard currencies of Europe during the years of Italian mercantilism, bore the image of John the Baptist on its face.

With the Medici family, these possible relationships with Hospitaller families seem even more obvious. For one thing, the name "Medici" itself implies ancestry from someone in the medical profession. For another, the Medicis' own family legend boasts of their descent from a mysterious knight of some unnamed order. As Jack Weatherford explains in *A History of Money*:

After coming to great power, the family claimed descent from a Knight Averado, who reputedly came to Italy on a pilgrimage to Rome but stopped in Tuscany long enough to slay a giant who had been terrorizing the peasants. The Holy Roman Emperor Charlemagne then supposedly awarded the brave knight a coat of arms bearing three red circles, representing the dents made in his shield by the giant. Some sources outside the family, however, claim that the three circles represent the three balls that have traditionally been the sign of the pawnbroker; others say they represent three coins.

The name Medici indicates descent from someone in the medical or pharmaceutical field, professions that were about equal in prestige to pawnbroking or barbering at that time. The three circles on the family's coat of arms may therefore represent pills, or the cupping glasses that doctors heated and applied to a patient's flesh in order to draw the 'bad blood' up to the skin's surface.

The Medicis were also connected to the royal and noble families ancestrally associated with the Knights Templar. You will recall how I mentioned in a previous chapter that the duke Rene d'Anjou had once employed both Christopher Columbus and Amerigo Vespucci, thus linking him inextricably to the movement to explore America. Rene d'Anjou was a descendant of Templar families as well, and is even believed to have been the Grand Master of a Templar splinter group called the Priory of Sion. In addition, Rene d'Anjou was connected to Cosimo de Medici, and was, like him, a pivotal figure in spreading the enlightened ideas of the Renaissance. Indeed, according to some authors, Rene d'Anjou may have been responsible for persuading Cosimo to undertake a lot of his influential activities. Michael Baigent, Richard Leigh and Henry Lincoln laid out this hypothesis in their bestseller, *Holy Blood, Holy Grail*:

It would not be inaccurate to regard Rene d'Anjou as a major impetus behind the phenomenon now called the Renaissance. Owing to his numerous Italian possessions he spent some years in Italy, and through his intimate friendship with the ruling Sforza family of Milan established contact with the Medicis of Florence. There is good reason to believe that it was largely Rene's influence that prompted Cosimo de Medici to embark on a series of ambitious projects – projects destined to transform Western Civilization.

Furthermore, this group, the Priory of Sion, is believed to have actually been in the possession of the head of Baphomet, which according to the

Priory's own documents, was given to them by the Templars in 1307, the year the Templars were disbanded. The head was referred to in the documents as the "Caput 58M" ("caput" being Latin for "head"), with the "M" written like the astrological symbol for Virgo (which looks very "M-like." One year prior in 1306, the Priory of Sion had adopted the subtitle "ORMUS." For their insignia, they chose the "M"-shaped Virgo symbol, inside of which they placed the other four letters of their new name: "O", "R", "U", and "S."

This name is very significant. For one thing, it was the name of a famous Egyptian alchemist from A.D. 46. It also stems from the name used for God in the Persian religion of Zoroastrianism, and for the wisdom principle in some Gnostic cults: "Ormuzd." It further contains the root word "or", which means "gold" in most European languages. All of this tends to indicate that the Priory of Sion anticipated receiving the Baphomet head, and believed that from it they would soon gain the ability to perform the alchemical task of turning dross into gold.

But at this point it may have seemed not to matter which group "possessed" the Baphomet, per se. With the Templars' invention of the check system and the later Italian improvements upon banking, the ability to create wealth was becoming less dependent upon the actually existence of precious metals or, indeed, any physical property. Thus, the ability to use the power of Baphomet may now have been less dependent upon the possession of a physical object. Perhaps after coming to possess the Mandylion, the Templars realized that the power of a copy or a representation of something (as money is of gold) can be equal to the power of the original, as long as it inspired the same faith.

At the same time, the old medieval Masonic guilds, which once revolved around the actual construction of buildings, now became based upon abstract ideas of philosophy. Thus was born Speculative Freemasonry, with the help of Templar-descended families who essentially turned this organization into a continuation of the Order of the Temple. Freemasonry, as we know, was perhaps *the* dominant influence on world events during the 1700s, as proto-Masonic/neo-Templar groups were during the 1500s and 1600s.

The early proto-Masonic occult circles of England came to be led, as I explained, in the 1600s by a visionary named Sir Francis Bacon. He was one of the founders of the Virginia Company, which first colonized the East Coast of North America for England. He also wrote *The New Atlantis*, a utopian fantasy in which he spelled out his vision for America as the site of the ultimate Masonic empire, directed by a cabal of enlightened intellectuals who called themselves, collectively, "Solomon's House." Francis Bacon and his friends were responsible for laying the groundwork for what was destined to come in 1776, and any secrets which the Templars might have possessed about statecraft or economics could have been passed along to the founders of the U.S. via this "Baconian Circle", as it has been called.

Indeed, many authors see the United States as an attempt by the Knights Templar to set up their own autonomous state – the ideal state, completely immune to religious and kingly authority, based upon enlightened philosophic principles, and made powerful with economics that the Templars invented, using the eternal hidden power of the universe symbolized by Baphomet. The only thing that one must bear in mind is that by the time the ideal Templar state was created, the Templars had become Freemasons.

In the next section, I explain how these principles are rooted in the ancient religious traditions of Christianity, Judaism, and pagan idol worship. I argue the following: that money has always been seen as being representative of both divine and royal power; that the coining of money has always been associated with the priesthood; that the operation of the economy has always been seen as metaphysical; that the tokens of money have always been thought of as enchanted objects; and that the gaining of wealth has often been viewed as being the result of allying oneself with divine or demonic powers. I also draw an interestingly link between America's wealth, King Solomon's treasure, and the famous "lost treasure of the Knights Templar." I think that this was not a vast horde of gold, but a formula for creating wealth. This formula was probably discovered by the Templars and passed on to certain Freemasons, who used it to construct the architecture of the US banking system.

PART III

Chapter Eleven:
The Temple of Money

The pursuit of money has long been thought to be at odds with the pursuit of spirituality. "Ye cannot serve both God and Mammon", Jesus says in the New Testament, "Mammon" being a Syriac word meaning "riches." We have seen that the Catholic Church has historically condemned the pursuit of wealth by individuals, although the pursuit of wealth by the Church itself has always been laudable and necessary. Similarly, the general religious attitude towards money is reflected in the almost universal prohibition against usury. The Judeo-Christian scriptures specifically prohibit it: *Leviticus 25:36-37* tells us: "Take thou no usury of him, or increase: but fear thy God; that thy brother may live with thee. Thou shalt not give him thy money upon usury, nor lend him thy victuals for increase." Similarly, we read in *Ezekiel 18:13*: "Hath given forth upon usury, and hath taken increase: shall he then live? he shall not live: he hath done all these abominations; he shall surely die; his blood shall be upon him."

While few churches or synagogues enforce these injunctions in modern times, Muslims still observe the prohibition against charging interest to another Muslim. Many Islamic countries find themselves in an economic straight-jacket because of this, and it would be fair to say that the standard of living in these countries might improve greatly if they would abandon it. Some financial institutions who do business in Islamic counties have found clever ways around the injunction, just as the merchants of Renaissance Venice and Florence found loopholes in the Catholic credo.

It may surprise some people, then, to learn that money actually has a religious origin. The oldest known coin currency that has been found is the Sumerian shekel, which dates from around 3000 B.C. It was created for use in a public religious rite known as "sacred prostitution." The priestesses of the fertility goddess Ishtar served her by offering themselves as representatives of her to male worshippers. It was thought that if the men simulated intercourse with the goddess, this would stimulate fertility in the land. A very important part of the ritual was the donation that occurred beforehand. The worshipper was expected to make offerings to the goddess in the form of wheat: the main agricultural product which they were asking the goddess to stimulate the production of.

During religious festivals, worshippers would bring a portion of their yearly wheat crop to the temple, where it was used to feed all of the priests, priestesses, and temple support staff. In exchange, they received one coin for each bushel of wheat, and each coin would entitle them to a visit with one of the priestesses. This is how the coin got its name: "shekel" means "bushel of wheat." The coin featured a sheaf of wheat on one side, and a depiction of Ishtar on the other. This identification of money with wheat continues into the present day, where words that translate as "bread" or "corn" are used as slang terms for money.

The origin of money in Greece was similar. Beginning in 1000 B.C., they minted coins as tokens given to the worshippers of Dionysus in exchange for the donation of a bull to the Dionysian temple. These bulls would all be sacrificed at the annual celebration known as the "sacred feast", to which Dionysus himself was invited. Half of the meat would be burned in honor of the god, while the rest was shared by the congregants – all those who could furnish a coin as proof of their donation.

As well, in contrast to the modern notion that "You can't take it with you", the Greeks believed that a deceased soul had to pay the ferryman, Charon, a fee for a ride down the river Styx to the underworld, Hades. Thus it was a tradition to place a coin under the tongue of a dead man. It was thought that if he did not have the fare for the ride, the man's soul would be lost in limbo, haunting the Earth forever. This tradition survived in the Western world into the early twentieth century, where it was customary to place *two* pennies on the eyelids of the deceased. (Note that even the economy of Hades is subject to inflation.)

When the large-scale minting of coins in Rome began in 269 B.C., this too had a connection to the divine. The new silver coin, called the "denarius" (root of the Spanish word for "money" - "dinero") was minted in the temple of the goddess Juno Moneta. This was the same Juno who was the wife of Jupiter, but she had been given the surname "Moneta", in much the same way that the Madonna is given specific appellations in Catholicism, named after various apparitions that she has made (Our Lady of Lourdes, etc). "Moneta" means "to warn", and its application to Juno stems from the following incident, described by Jack Weatherford in *A History of Money*:

As an extension of her role as protector of women and guardian of the family, Juno became the patroness of the Roman state. According to Roman historians, in the fourth century B.C., the irritated honking of the sacred geese around Juno's temple on Capitoline Hill warned the people of an impending night attack by the Gauls, who were secretly scaling the walls of the citadel.

We should note that as the wife of Jupiter, the most high god of the Romans, Juno was the most high goddess, the Queen of Heaven, and thus was essentially equivalent to the Greek Hera, wife of Zeus, or to the Eastern goddess, Ishtar. You will recall that in a previous chapter I described the phenomenon of political states throughout history identifying themselves with a national goddess figure (Columbia for the Americans, Britannia for the British, Marianne for the French, etc). Juno played that role for the Romans, who saw her as the protectress of the state. Thus, the issuance of money was one of the activities in Rome that she was thought to preside over. It is from Juno's surname of "Moneta" that the English words "money", "monetary", and "mint" are derived. Jack Weatherford notes that there are similar words in many other languages, and also mentions the fact that the use of these words continues the ancient association between money and the goddess. He writes:

Cognates in other European languages also derive from 'moneta', including the Spanish 'moneda', meaning 'coin.' From very early classical times, money showed a close relationship to the divine and to the female. We can still see that connection in money-related words in European languages, which are frequently feminine in gender, as in the Spanish 'la moneda' and the German 'die Mark' and 'die Munze' (coin).

In addition, there were a number of ancient societies who valued gold and silver, even before they learned to use it for money, because they associated it with their main god and goddess, the Sun and the Moon. Juno and Jupiter, as well as Hera and Zeus, were lunar and solar deities, with the male god representing the Sun, and his wife representing the Moon. The same associations were made in almost all ancient cultures, and as Jack Weatherford explains, they often made religious offerings of silver and gold to their gods and goddesses:

In particular, gold was considered a divine substance. People around the world noted the resemblance of the color to the sun, a coincidence to which they ascribed a deeper meaning. The ancient Egyptians believed that gold was sacred to Ra, the sun god, and they buried great quantities of it with the corpses of their divine pharaohs. Among the Incas of South America, gold and silver represented the sweat of the sun and the moon, and they covered the walls of their temples with these precious metals. Even after conquest, when the Spaniards took the Indian gold and silver, the natives decorated their new Christian temples with foil paper to imitate the sacred substances, and they tossed gold- and silver-colored confetti into the air in place of gold dust. The ancient people of India considered gold the sacred semen of Agni, the fire god; therefore they donated gold for any service performed by Agni's priests.

In his thorough examination of ancient customs, *Atlantis: The Antediluvian World*, Ignatius Donnelly surmised why gold was valued by the ancients so much more than silver:

...as the reverence for the great burning orb of the sun, master of all the manifestations of nature, was tenfold as great as the veneration for the smaller, weaker, and variable goddess of the night, so was the demand for the metal sacred to the sun ten times as great as for the metal sacred to the moon. This view is confirmed by the fact that the root of the word by which the Celts, the Greeks, and the Romans designated gold was the Sanscrit word karat, which means, 'the color of the sun.'

Donnelly then draws our attention to a fascinating custom among the English which demonstrates that the association between the Moon and silver has survived into the modern era:

In England, to this day the new moon is saluted with a bow or a courtesy, as well as the curious practice of 'turning one's silver,' which seems a relic of the offering of the moon's proper metal. The custom of wishing, when one first sees the new moon, is probably a survival of moon-worship; the wish taking the place of the prayer.

Another author, Bernard Lietaer, in his book *The Future of Money: Creating New Wealth, Work and a Wiser World*, introduces anecdotal evidence which tends to indicate that there is something intrinsic in nature that does indeed link these metals with their respective heavenly bodies. As he states:

Many centuries later, without the need for further clerical intervention, gold and silver remained respectively symbolically associated with the sun and the moon. Their prices settled mysteriously into a stable ratio of 1/13.5, astrologically determined to reflect the heavenly cycles.

What he means regarding the heavenly cycles is that there are thirteen lunar cycles for every solar year, and in a lunar year (thirteen cycles of twenty-eight days each), there are 364 days. Thus the Moon, and by extension, silver, is linked symbolically with the number 13. More evidence of a link between silver and the Moon comes from *A Beginner's*

Guide to Constructing the Universe: The Mathematical Archetypes of Nature, Art, and Science, by Michael S. Schneider, where he writes:

Just as gold is the metal whose color, and inability to tarnish, has traditionally associated it with the sun, silver is linked with the moon. Indeed, on a clear night in the country the moon appears quite silvery. The ancients chose a symbol more appropriate than they may have known. It was only in this century that scientists probing the atom found that the atomic weight of silver, its weight relative to carbon, is 107.870, or nearly 108, a tenth of the moon's radius of 1080 miles.

There was another ancient culture which also used precious metals for religious purposes, and they are directly related to our inquiry. I am speaking of the ancient Jews and Israelites of the Holy Land. The origin of money in ancient Israel was the same as with all civilizations of antiquity: it originated with the priesthood.

Chapter Twelve:
The Iniquity of Priesthood

In Old Testament times, the practice of priesthood in the kingdoms of Judah and Israel was restricted to those of the tribe of Levi. Every single male Levite was required to serve in the priesthood. That was the only occupation allowed to him. This was a circumstance demanded by God himself, who had personally stipulated not only that all priests should be Levites, and all Levites priests, but that the priests should also be barred from owning property. Their only source of income was the tithes and other offerings given to them by the people of Israel in exchange for their priestly services. The people were obliged to give ten percent of their own earnings to the priesthood, and often paid for each priestly duty performed as well. But the Levites were not allowed to own any land, and while the other eleven tribes each had their own territory within Israel, the Levites were obliged to live scattered throughout the other territories, sometimes in public-owned housing, in or near the centers of religious worship, and sometimes as guests at the houses of certain wealthy families who could afford to hire a personal priest.

The Old Testament is very clear about the fact that service in God's priesthood was, more than anything else, a burden. As it states in *Numbers 18*:

And the LORD said unto Aaron, Thou and thy sons and thy father's house with thee shall bear the iniquity of the sanctuary: and thou and thy sons with thee shall bear the iniquity of your priesthood....And I, behold, I have taken your brethren the Levites from among the children of Israel: to you they are given as a gift for the LORD, to do the service of the tabernacle of the congregation....

But the Levites shall do the service of the tabernacle of the congregation, and they shall bear their iniquity: it shall be a statute for ever throughout your generations, that among the children of Israel they have no inheritance. But the tithes of the children of Israel, which they offer as an heave offering unto the LORD, I have given to the Levites to inherit: therefore I have said unto them, Among the children of Israel they shall have no inheritance.

And the LORD spake unto Moses, saying, Thus speak unto the Levites, and say unto them, When ye take of the children of Israel the tithes which I have given you from them for your inheritance, then ye shall offer up an heave offering of it for the LORD, even a tenth part of the tithe.

The Levites were chosen for the priesthood partially as a punishment for the behavior of their progenitor, Levi, who, along with his brother Simeon, had waged a genocidal war on the nation of Shechem, against the wishes of Jehovah, and of their father, Jacob. This led Jacob to pronounce a curse upon the two sons when he was on his deathbed. He stated:

Simeon and Levi are brethren; instruments of cruelty are in their habitations. O my soul, come not thou into their secret; unto their assembly, mine honour, be not thou united: for in their anger they slew a man, and in their selfwill they digged down a wall. Cursed be their anger, for it was fierce; and their wrath, for it was cruel: I will divide them in Jacob, and scatter them in Israel.

However, it was not until the Exodus that God cursed them with the iniquity of priesthood. On the night of the first Passover, God slaughtered the firstborn of every house in Egypt. But he passed over the houses of the Hebrews, who had painted the doors of their houses with lamb's blood at the command of God. Thus did the angel of death know to leave those houses alone. Yet in exchange for sparing the firstborn of the Hebrews, God demanded a substitute sacrifice. The sons of the tribe of Levi were chosen as the substitute, and although they were allowed to continue living, their inheritance, which every other tribe descended from Jacob's sons had been blessed with, was taken away from them. Moses and Aaron (both Levites) led the Hebrews out of Egypt and initiated an everlasting covenant between God and the Hebrews, in which they would pay homage and sacrifice to God in exchange for his protection. The Levites were then called to the priesthood, to be the mediators of this contract.

In a sense, the Levites became the most powerful people in Israel, and yet they had no property. They were the scapegoats who took on the ultimate responsibility. If the people of Israel sinned against God, then God would punish the people in general, but would punish the Levites foremost for failing to properly lead. And if God punished the people of Israel, then the people blamed the priests for failing to secure God's favor. Thus the Levite priests endured much, and wholly earned the tithes that they received. The tithes were not considered gifts, but rather payment for services rendered, and the priests used what they were given not only for religious activities, but for their own personal needs as well. This was considered not a potential corrupting influence, but as a bulwark against corruption, for a well-paid priesthood was less likely to accept bribes to perform impious deeds.

Nevertheless, the priests of Israel often did indulge in impious deeds, by accepting money or other donations in exchange for performing rites to heathen gods. And although God may have looked down upon such behavior, it was considered quite normal in Israel, especially when times were hard financially. In Louis Ginzberg's *The Legends of the Jews*, the author writes about a certain Levite priest, the grandson of Moses, who learned from his grandfather that if a priest could not earn an acceptable living serving God, it was better to supplement one's income by serving heathen gods for heathen clients, rather than begging for handouts from fellow Israelites. As Ginzberg writes:

From his grandfather he had heard the rule that a man should do 'Abodah Zarah' for hire rather than be dependent upon his fellow-creatures. The meaning of 'Abodah Zarah' here naturally is 'strange', in the sense of 'unusual' work, but he took the term in its ordinary acceptation of 'service of strange gods.'

Perhaps because heathen religious rituals often involved the rites of "sacred prostitution", as previously described, with the use of "temple prostitutes" who were paid for their services, the worship of strange gods is often referred to in the Old Testament as "whoring." And in heathen religions, as in the Judaic tradition, there was quite a significance placed on the relationship between the service of the priests and the money they were paid to perform it. Simply put, the tithes paid to the priests, along with the prayers, animal sacrifices, and other rituals, in a way, provided the power and spiritual energy upon which the priesthood operated. The money paid by the congregation to the priests was a financial sacrifice to the god(s) they were servicing.

This is illustrated by the fact that heathen rites often involved the worship of religious idols which were made out of gold and silver that had been donated to the cause, sometimes by members of the congregation. In *The Book of Judges*, we read about Micah, the Levite priest descended from Moses discussed earlier, who performed "strange service" for Israelites with heathen beliefs. Micah held services with a handful of religious idols that he had crafted out of silver which had been donated by his mother Delilah specifically for this cause. By donating this silver, she was providing a seed upon which Micah's lucrative priesthood would grow, for he would then charge believing heathens money to perform rites on their behalf in homage to these idols. The same principle was illustrated in the story of the golden calf in *Exodus*, which was fashioned by the high priest Aaron out of the golden jewelry donated by the people who worshipped it. Thus it "contained", spiritually, their covenant with Belial, the deity it represented - a covenant bought with the price of that gold, which is why Moses had them drink the gold as a punishment - to internalize the curse which God had placed upon them for worshipping the calf.

Chapter Thirteen:
A Trespass Offering

There is another story in the Old Testament which illustrates a similar principle as that found in the golden calf story. It is the story of the plague at Ashdod told in *I Samuel 4 – 6*. When Israel was at war with the Philistines, there was an incident in which the enemy actually managed to capture the Ark of the Covenant. They took it to Ashdod and set it up in the Temple of Dagon, their god of wisdom, placing it right next to the great statue of Dagon that was there. The next day, however, the Philistines awoke to a surprise. *I Samuel 5:3 – 5* states:

And when they arose early on the morrow morning, behold, Dagon was fallen upon his face to the ground before the ark of the LORD; and the head of Dagon and both the palms of his hands were cut off upon the threshold; only the stump of Dagon was left to him. Therefore neither the priests of Dagon, nor any that come into Dagon's house, tread on the threshold of Dagon in Ashdod unto this day. But the hand of the LORD was heavy upon them of Ashdod, and he destroyed them, and smote them with emerods, even Ashdod and the coasts thereof.

These "emerods" appear to be bubonic tumors, a punishment brought by God to the Philistines for defiling the Holy Ark. The Philistines found that everywhere they tried to bring the Ark, a plague of "emerods" broke out. *I Samuel 5:7 – 11* says:

And when the men of Ashdod saw that it was so, they said, The ark of the God of Israel shall not abide with us: for his hand is sore upon us, and upon Dagon our god. They sent therefore and gathered all the lords of the Philistines unto them, and said, What shall we do with the ark of the God of Israel? And they answered, Let the ark of the God of Israel be carried about unto Gath. And they carried the ark of the God of Israel about thither. And it was so, that, after they had carried it about, the hand of the LORD was against the city with a very great destruction: and he smote the men of the city, both small and great, and they had emerods in their secret parts. Therefore they sent the ark of God to Ekron. And it came to pass, as the ark of God came to Ekron, that the Ekronites cried out, saying, They have brought about the ark of the God of Israel to us, to slay us and our people. So they sent and gathered together all the lords of the Philistines, and said, Send away the ark of the God of Israel, and let it go again to his own place, that it slay us not, and our people: for there was a deadly destruction throughout all the city; the hand of God was very heavy there.

After consulting with their oracles, the priests of the Philistines decided to return the Ark to the Israelites, hoping that this would end the plague. Also, to ward off any future bad karma, they decided to make a "trespass offering", an "I'm sorry" gift to the God of Israel. The priests instructed the Philistines to make golden replicas of the emerods they had been smitten with, as well as effigies of the mice that, presumably, had carried the plague everywhere the Ark went. *I Samuel 6: 3-8* quotes the priests as saying:

...If ye send away the ark of the God of Israel, send it not empty; but in any wise return him a trespass offering: then ye shall be healed, and it shall be known to you why his hand is not removed from you. Then said they, What shall be the trespass offering which we shall return to him? They answered, Five golden emerods, and five golden mice, according to the number of the lords of the Philistines: for one plague was on you all, and on your lords. Wherefore ye shall make images of your emerods, and images of your mice that mar the land; and ye shall give glory unto the God of Israel: peradventure he will lighten his hand from off you, and from off your gods, and from off your land. ... Now therefore make a new cart, and take two milch kine, on which there hath come no yoke, and tie the kine to the cart, and bring their calves home from them: And take the ark of the LORD, and lay it upon the cart; and put the jewels of gold, which ye return him for a trespass offering, in a coffer by the side thereof; and send it away, that it may go.

Thus we see that the Philistines believed gold was a fitting offering to a foreign god. They also believed that using that gold to make representations of their afflictions would cure them of it, if these representations were offered to the god whom they believed to be causing their afflictions.

A fascinating side note is that the Philistine town in which this all started, Ashdod, has been changed in many European renderings to "Azoth." For instance, when the French painter Nicolas Poussin portrayed the incident, he titled his work *La Peste d'Azoth*. The "Azoth" is also a code name for the alchemical element of Mercury. It actually represents the idea of totality because it starts with "A", which is the first letter in most alphabets, and end with "z", "o," and "th", which are the final letters of the Latin, Greek, and Hebrew alphabets. It was thought by some alchemists in Renaissance Europe (those who studied the teachings of an alchemical sage named Paracelsus) that the "Azoth" was a cure for syphilis, which they believed was the true nature of the plague at

Ashdod. Nicholas Poussin was such a follower of Paracelsus, as explained by Sheila Barker in her article "Poussin, plague, and early modern medicine" in the December 2004 edition of *The Art Bulletin*:

Given Poussin's contact with a Paracelsan adherent in the years preceding The Plague of Ashdod, it should also be mentioned that in certain learned circles, Azoth, French for Ashdod, signified more than just the city of the Philistines. Azoth was the name of the kabbalistic sign for the mercury principle in alchemical operations; it was a name for the mercury (argento vivo, quicksilver) cautiously recommended by both Paracelsus and Potier as an effective but dangerous remedy for syphilis; and it was the secret name of Paracelsus's famous panacea ('Azoth of the Red Lion'), extracted from cinnabar and associated with the alchemistic philosopher's stone. This last significance is laid out in medical writings including Potier's Pharmacopoea spagirica and his De febribus, as well as in esoteric writings such as Jacques Nuysement's 'Philosophical Poem on the Philosophers' Azoth' and a late sixteenth-century pseudo-Paracelsan treatise that identifies this substance, 'AZOT,' as the 'arcanum sanctum' (the secret of secrets) and associates it etymologically with the kabbalistic theme of the Ark of the Israelites - the same as that seen in Poussin's picture.

The idea of the "trespass offering" was not unique to the Philistines. The Israelites likewise made these offerings to their God, whenever they sinned against him, in an effort to appease him. The most important such offering was that which was made on behalf of the whole kingdom, in the form of the scapegoat sacrifice on Yom Kippur, the Day of Atonement. The ritual is described in *Leviticus 16*, in which two goats are sacrificed, one of which (the Scapegoat) is literally cursed with the blame of all of the people's sins for the entire year. Interestingly, the word used to identify the Scapegoat is "Azazel", the name of a Middle Eastern goat deity who is yet another candidate that has been proposed for the Baphomet, and his name is reminiscent of "Azoth."

Later, especially after the destruction of the Temple of Solomon, trespass offerings would be made mainly in cash.

Chapter Fourteen:
The Shekel of the Sanctuary

The payment of tithes to the priesthood of Israel, and to their royal government as well, became a major part of the lifestyle of the ancient Israelites. Either way, whether received by the king or the priesthood, tithes were considered sacrifices unto the Lord himself. The first recording of the practice in the Bible is in *Genesis*, where Abraham gave a tenth of his possessions as a donation to the priest-king of Salem, Melchizedek. In *Genesis 28:22*, Jacob promised God that he would give "the tenth" after his divine vision at Bethel, which led to him building a temple of God there. But tithing developed over time into a rather complex system, as described by The Catholic Encyclopedia, (http://www.newadvent.org/cathen/), tithing is:

Generally defined as 'the tenth part of the increase arising from the profits of land and stock, allotted to the clergy for their support or devoted to religious or charitable uses.' A more radical definition is 'the tenth part of all fruits and profits justly acquired, owed to God in recognition of his supreme dominion over man, and to be paid to the ministers of the church.' ... Under the Mosaic Law the payment of tithes was made obligatory. The Hebrews are commanded to offer to God the tenth part of the produce of the fields, of the fruits of the trees, and the firstborn of oxen and of sheep (Lev., xxvii, 30; Deut., xiv, 22). In Deuteronomy there is a mention not only of an annual tithe, but also of a full tithe to be paid once every three years. While it was to God Himself that the tithes had to be paid, yet we read (Num., xviii, 21) that He transfers them to His sacred ministers: 'I have given to the sons of Levi all the tithes of Israel for a possession, for the ministry wherewith they serve me in the tabernacle of the covenant.' In paying the tithe, the Hebrews divided the annual harvest into ten parts, one of which was given to the Levites after the first-fruits had been subtracted. This was partitioned by them among the priests. The remainder of the harvest was then divided into ten new parts, and a second tithe was carried by the head of the household to the sanctuary to serve as a sacred feast for his family and the Levites.

If the journey to the temple was unusually long, money could be substituted for the offering in kind. At the triennial tithe, a third decimation was made and a tenth part was consumed at home by the householder with his family, the Levites, strangers, and the poor. This triennial year was called the year of tithes (Deut., xxvi, 12). As the tithes were the main support of the priests, it was later ordained that the offerings should be stored in the temple (II Par., xxxi, 11).

The Catholic Encyclopedia then goes on to point out that tithing was widespread throughout the ancient world – not just offering donations of the priesthood, but specifically donating a tenth of one's holdings. They offer the following analysis:

The explanation of why the tenth part should have been chosen among so many different peoples is said to be (apart from a common primitive revelation) that mystical signification of the number ten, viz., that it signifies totality, for it contains all the numbers that make up the numerical system, and indeed all imaginable series of numbers, and so it represents all kinds of property, which is a gift to God. All species of property were consequently reckoned in decades, and by consecrating one of these parts to God, the proprietor recognized the Source of his goods.

In addition to these tithes, a tax was instituted among the Israelites to support the upkeep of the Tabernacle, when it was built to house the Ark of the Covenant. When God instructed Moses on how to build the Ark, the Tabernacle, and all of the other priestly accoutrements, He told Moses that the materials had to be donated by the Israelites. As he explains in *Exodus 25: 1-8*:

And the LORD spake unto Moses, saying. Speak unto the children of Israel, that they bring me an offering: of every man that giveth it willingly with his heart ye shall take my offering. And this is the offering which ye shall take of them; gold, and silver, and brass, And blue, and purple, and scarlet, and fine linen, and goats' hair. And rams' skins dyed red, and badgers' skins, and shittim wood. Oil for the light, spices for anointing oil, and for sweet incense. Onyx stones, and stones to be set in the ephod, and in the breastplate. And let them make me a sanctuary; that I may dwell among them.

This is yet another example of the ancient idea that members of any particular cult must donate the materials used to craft their idols and places of worship. Notice that gold is the primary material used, being the most appropriate gift to honor a god.

The Lord goes on to explain to Moses the exact "pattern" to use when constructing each item – indicating that there was something sacred about every detail of the dimensions of these objects, the materials used, and the manner in which they were obtained. The Tabernacle was made to house the Ark, in which the spirit of the Lord was believed to literally reside. Inside of this Ark the Tablets of Testimony were also placed, written by the very finger of God, detailing the contract between God and the Israelites that was being continued with the priestly services performed in the Tabernacle.

In the next few passages, God describes at length how the Levites should take a census of the Israelites every year, and tax them all a half-shekel each, "after the shekel of the sanctuary." Yes, like the Sumerians and other ancient peoples, the Israelites called their currency the "shekel." *Exodus 30:12 -16* states

When thou takest the sum of the children of Israel after their number, then shall they give every man a ransom for his soul unto the LORD, when thou numberest them; that there be no plague among them, when thou numberest them. This they shall give, every one that passeth among them that are numbered, half a shekel after the shekel of the sanctuary: (a shekel is twenty gerahs:) an half shekel shall be the offering of the LORD. Every one that passeth among them that are numbered, from twenty years old and above, shall give an offering unto the LORD. The rich shall not give more, and the poor shall not give less than half a shekel, when they give an offering unto the LORD, to make an atonement for your souls. And thou shalt take the atonement money of the children of Israel, and shalt appoint it for the service of the tabernacle of the congregation; that it may be a memorial unto the children of Israel before the LORD, to make an atonement for your souls.

The phrase "shekel of the Sanctuary" is used repeatedly throughout the Pentateuch, and refers to the fact that the standard weight for Israelite shekels was to be measured and assayed (tested) within the Tabernacle by the Levites, as it later would be in the Temple of Solomon. The shekel's weight was actually related mathematically to the size of the Israelite cubit, the standard of which was extracted from the measurements of the Holy of Holies, the 20 cubit by 20 cubit by 20 cubit perfect cube in the center of the Tabernacle, in which the Ark was kept, and in which only the High Priest Aaron and his sons were allowed to step foot.

But when people speak of "the Sanctuary" and the "Holy of Holies" now, they are usually referring not to the Tabernacle, but to King Solomon's Temple, the crowning achievement of Israel. It would become not only the house of God, and the center of an empire, but a symbol of wisdom and wealth in perfection to future Jews, Christians, Templars, and Freemasons.

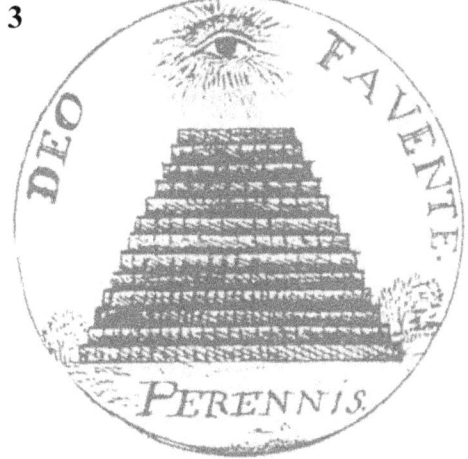

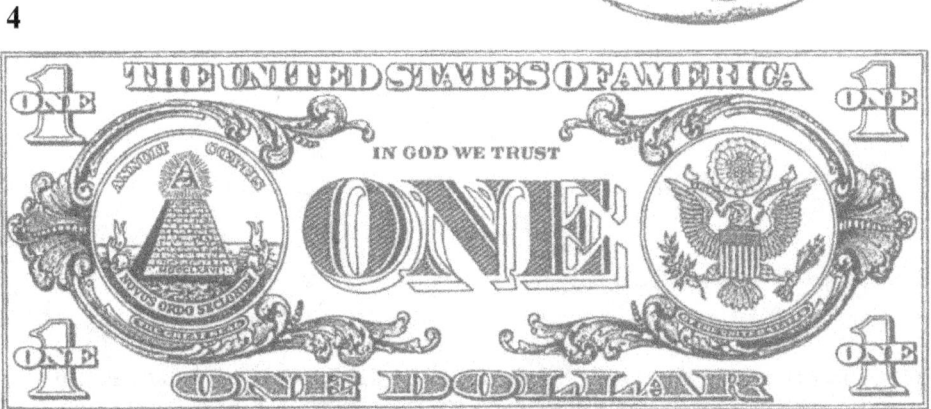

(1) The front and back of the Great Seal of the United States. **(2)** Motif from a banknote for one third of a dollar, designed by William Barton. **(3)** Alternate design for the Great Seal, by William Barton. **(4)** The back of the modern US one dollar bill.

5

6

7

8

9

10

(5) Copper coin from Vermont, 1785, featuring the All-Seeing Eye, 13 stars, and 26 rays. **(6)** Early American coin featuring the goddess Columbia. **(7)** American dime featuring the bust of Mercury, or Hermes. **(8)** The caduceus. **(9)** A common form of the caduceus, a serpent on a tau cross, could be the origin of the dollar sign, according to David Ovason. **(10)** Ovason also notes that the alchemical sign for Mercury is very similar to the dollar sign.

(11) Spanish silver dollars depicting the Pillars of Hercules and the motto "Plus Ultra." (12) Ancient coin from Tyre featuring the Pillars of Hercules and the serpent in the Tree of Knowledge, another possible origin for the dollar sign. (13) *America and the Federal Reserve Board*, by John Gregory, which shows Columbia sporting a caduceus, with the Federal Reserve seal as her shield.

14

15

(14) Another seal designed by William Barton, showing Columbia holding a dove.
(15) This illustration of the Exchequer of Ireland at work shows the use of a chequerboard as an abacus in the thirteenth and fourteenth centuries.

(16) Masonic device featuring a broken column, a weeping virgin, a sprig of acacia, and Father Time. It symbolizes the loss of the secrets of Solomon's Temple.

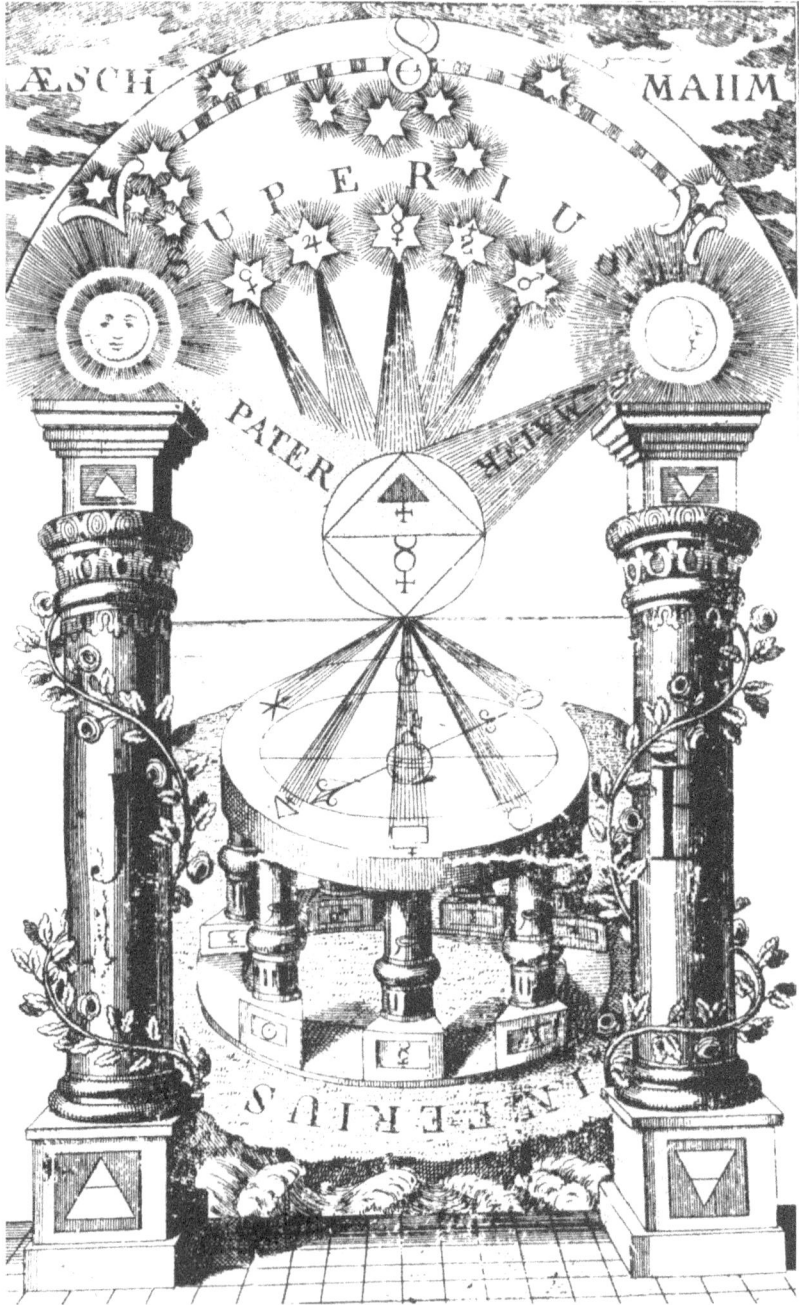

(17) From an anonymous German alchemical tract *The Compass of the Wise*, a drawing showing the pillars of Jachin and Boaz, each swathed in vines.

(18) The seal of the Knights Templar, depicting two knights riding on a single horse. **(19)** Greek Orthodox icon believed to be a replica of the Mandylion. **(20)** A contemporary illustration of the execution of Templar Grand Master Jacques de Molay in 1314.

(21) The "Goat of Mendes" symbol used by the Church of Satan. **(22)** The famous drawing of Baphomet by Eliphas Levi.

23

24  **25**

26

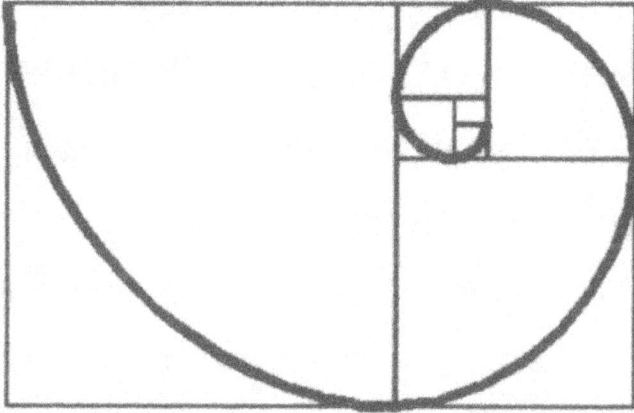

(23) The skull and crossbones, or Jolly Roger. **(24)** The Chi Rho symbol envisioned by Constantine. **(25)** The Fibonacci spiral with the pentagram. **(26)** The Fibonacci spiral within a golden triangle.

(27) *The Plague of Ashdod*, or *La Peste d'Azoth*, by Nicolas Poussin.

28

29   **30**

31   **32**

(28) The front and back of the Tyrian shekel, which resembles the American quarter-dollar coin. **(29)** An Israelite shekel. **(30)** Hexagonal geometry on the front of the Great Seal of the United States, as revealed by author Michael Schneider. **(31)** Statue of George Washington by Horatio Greenough, depicting him in a Baphometic pose. **(32)** A Masonic device showing the two Saints John: the Baptist on the left, and the Evangelist on the right. The Baptist strikes the Baphometic pose.

34

$$= \triangleleft + O + \frown + \triangleright + \smile + \text{|}$$

$$= \frac{1}{2} + \frac{1}{4} + \frac{1}{8} + \frac{1}{16} + \frac{1}{32} + \frac{1}{64}$$

35

36

(34) The Wedjat eye and its six parts, which were used by Egyptians as symbols of mathematical fractions. (35) An Egyptian depiction of the Wedjat eye hovering over an arch. (36) A hieroglyph showing the Wedjat eye in conjunction with a chequerboard pattern.

Chapter Fifteen:
King Solomon's Temple

Wisdom, wealth, and the building of the Temple are the three things that King Solomon is best known for. The wisdom he acquired from God himself, when he went before the Ark of the Covenant to pray. *II Chronicles* starts off with this story, telling us in Chapter 1:6-12 that:

...Solomon went up thither to the brazen altar before the LORD, which was at the tabernacle of the congregation, and offered a thousand burnt offerings upon it. In that night did God appear unto Solomon, and said unto him, Ask what I shall give thee. And Solomon said unto God, Thou hast shewed great mercy unto David my father, and hast made me to reign in his stead. Now, O LORD God, let thy promise unto David my father be established: for thou hast made me king over a people like the dust of the earth in multitude. Give me now wisdom and knowledge, that I may go out and come in before this people: for who can judge this thy people, that is so great?

God was impressed with the pious and humble nature of Solomon's request. Given the option to be granted anything he wished, he chose wisdom! Because of this, God blessed Solomon even beyond what he had requested:

And God said to Solomon, Because this was in thine heart, and thou hast not asked riches, wealth, or honour, nor the life of thine enemies, neither yet hast asked long life; but hast asked wisdom and knowledge for thyself, that thou mayest judge my people, over whom I have made thee king: Wisdom and knowledge is granted unto thee; and I will give thee riches, and wealth, and honour, such as none of the kings have had that have been before thee, neither shall there any after thee have the like.

It was after God invested him with this wisdom that Solomon started becoming very wealthy, collecting chariots and horses, importing exotic linens and spices, jewels, gold and silver, and numerous other luxury items. In particular, *II Chronicles* says that he "made silver and gold at Jerusalem as plenteous as stones." He then became obsessed with a mission that he had inherited from his father David: to build a spectacular temple to house the Ark of God, instead of the tent that it had heretofore been sitting in. He also wanted to build an extravagant royal palace for himself and his many wives. *II Chronicles* treats the creation of these two buildings as one event, whereas *I Kings*, which also tells the story of Solomon, specifies that he spent the first seven years building the temple, and then the next thirteen years building the royal palace. Nevertheless, they were both part of the same overall architectural compound. *II Chronicles* details how Solomon reached out to the King of Tyre, Hiram (called "Huram" in *II Chronicles*), who had previously been an ally of his father David.

Hiram was also wealthy and wise, and ruled over a powerful Phoenician island city-state, which at the time held a vast empire with numerous colonies, and was the center of the world's merchant economy. They had colonies in Greece, Northern Africa, Carthage, Sicily, Corsica, and Spain. The word "Tyre" is actually a Latinization of the name of this city. It was called in the Phoenician tongue "Assur", or "Sur", as the natives who live there still call it. The word means "rock", and is connected to the name of the later people known as the "Assyrians", as well as the modern Syrians. When Tyre was dominant, most of the Phoenicians or, as they termed themselves, "Canaanites", were also loosely called "Tyrians" by the outside world, or else, "Sidonians", after another Phoenician city, Sidon.

All collectively termed "the Sea Peoples" by historians, the Phoenicians were sea-farers and merchants. The word "Canaanite" became a more generalized international term for "merchant." Meanwhile, "Phoenician" is a term that is derived from one of the region's chief exports, a purple dye made from snails that was highly valued for coloring textiles, specifically those made to be worn by royalty. (The color has been associated with royalty ever since.) "Phoenix" also became the name of a mythical bird, which purportedly was able to live 500 years and then died, only to be reborn from the ashes of her own funeral pyre. This bird became a symbol of alchemy, and was employed by the Freemasons. (You will recall that Manly P. Hall believed the eagle on the back of the Great Seal of the U.S. was meant to covertly represent a phoenix.)

The Phoenicians developed an alphabet (technically called an "abjad" because it contains no vowels), which they developed for use in trade. This 22-letter abjad formed the basis of the Greek alphabet and, in an indirect way, all those of the Middle East and India. The major goddess worshipped by the Sea Peoples, Astarte, is probably related to the Phoenician name of Tyre, "Assur." Their main god, known as "Baal" or "Melqart", became united over time in their minds with the Greek figure of Hercules. In King Hiram's time, there was a magnificent temple of Melqart which dominated the island, and outside of the entrance to the temple were two massive pillars, representing the Pillars of Hercules. This temple became the blueprint for the one that Solomon was to have built.

Solomon and Hiram had a close friendship and business relationship, which was a continuation of a friendship between Hiram and David. *II Chronicles, 2:3* states:

... Solomon sent to Huram the king of Tyre, saying, As thou didst deal with David my father, and didst send him cedars to build him an house to dwell therein, even so deal with me.

The Tyrians did indeed provide lumber for the building of King David's royal palace. But there was more going on in this new relationship between Solomon and Hiram than just the continuation of a hereditary alliance. They were forming a new bond. *I Kings 5:12* describes it thusly:

And the LORD gave Solomon wisdom, as he promised him: and there was peace between Hiram and Solomon; and they two made a league together.

The phrasing of this is interesting, as though the diplomatic relations between Hiram and Solomon were a *result* of the wisdom that he obtained from God. At any rate, the word "league" is defined by *Webster's Dictionary* as "a covenant or compact made between persons, parties, states, etc., for the promotion or maintenance of common interests or for mutual assistance or service. This is what Hiram and Solomon had together, and this is why their relationship serves as an example of the ideal fraternal bond in the rituals of Freemasonry. The league between Solomon and Hiram was formed when Hiram agreed to help provide materials, architects, and workmen to Hiram for the building of Solomon's temple, in exchange for certain provisions. *I Kings 5:8-11* says:

... Hiram sent to Solomon, saying, I have considered the things which thou sentest to me for: and I will do all thy desire concerning timber of cedar, and concerning timber of fir. My servants shall bring them down from Lebanon unto the sea: and I will convey them by sea in floats unto the place that thou shalt appoint me, and will cause them to be discharged there, and thou shalt receive them: and thou shalt accomplish my desire, in giving food for my household. So Hiram gave Solomon cedar trees and fir trees according to all his desire. And Solomon gave Hiram twenty thousand measures of wheat for food to his household, and twenty measures of pure oil: thus gave Solomon to Hiram year by year.

The reason why the Tyrians needed these things from the Israelites was because the Phoenicians were not very good at conducting their own agriculture, since their land was non-arable. Necessity being the mother of invention, the Phoenicians developed sophisticated trade networks and practices that gained them enough wealth and power to obtain everything else they needed or wanted. Also, luck had positioned them in the middle of the trade routes between Mesopotamia, Arabia and Egypt. They were able to use this strategic position as leverage to impose their own trade agreements on the surrounding nations.

The agreement the Tyrians made with Solomon began with the building of the Temple, but quickly grew into a much larger trading partnership that greatly expanded the wealth and territories of Israel. The Tyrians even allowed Israel to make use of their shipping fleet. Clearly Solomon's wisdom was guiding him on how to create a vibrant economy.

In every way, the Temple reflected the concept of extravagant wealth, and of its continual growth. The materials used in building the temple were extremely valuable: the cedars of Lebanon, expensive cloth dyed with Tyre's famous purple, and lots of gold. Furthermore, every item was crafted by the best in the world, the Phoenicians, most especially the architecture of the Temple itself. The Sea Peoples were among the ancient world's most accomplished temple-builders.

In the rituals of Freemasonry, there are two "Hirams" who each play a role in their rituals regarding the building of Solomon's Temple. One is Hiram, the king of Tyre, and the other they call "Hiram Abiff", referring to another figure mentioned in both *II Chronicles* and *I Kings*, who was a master architect sent by Hiram of Tyre to direct the building of Solomon's Temple. In *II Chronicles, Chapter 2: 13-14*, King Hiram writes a letter to Solomon about a man that his father (*also* named "Hiram", or "Huram") knows, who is a good architect, and promises to dispatch him to help with the Temple. The text states:

And now I have sent a cunning man, endued with understanding, of Huram my father's, The son of a woman of the daughters of Dan, and his father was a man of Tyre, skilful to work in gold, and in silver, in brass, in iron, in stone, and in timber, in purple, in blue, and in fine linen, and in crimson; also to grave any manner of graving, and to find out every device which shall be put to him, with thy cunning men, and with the cunning men of my lord David thy father.

Elsewhere, in *II Chronicles, Chapter 4:11 – 4:18*, it sounds as if this architect is *yet also* named "Hiram" or ("Huram"):

And Huram made the pots, and the shovels, and the basins. And Huram finished the work that he was to make for king Solomon for the house of God; To wit, the two pillars, and the pommels, and the chapiters which were on the top of the two pillars, and the two wreaths to cover the two pommels of the chapiters which were on the top of the pillars; And four hundred pomegranates on the two wreaths; two rows of pomegranates on each wreath, to cover the two pommels of the chapiters which were upon the pillars. He made also bases, and lavers made he upon the bases; One sea, and twelve oxen under it. The pots also, and the shovels, and the fleshhooks, and all their instruments, did Huram his father make to king Solomon for the house of the LORD of bright brass. In the plain of Jordan did the king cast them, in the clay ground between Succoth and Zeredathah. Thus Solomon made all these vessels in great abundance: for the weight of the brass could not be found out.

This notion that the very architect of Solomon's Temple was also named Hiram is backed up by *I Kings, Chapter 7:13-7:22*, which says:

And king Solomon sent and fetched Hiram out of Tyre. He was a widow's son of the tribe of Naphtali, and his father was a man of Tyre, a worker in brass: and he was filled with wisdom, and understanding, and cunning to work all works in brass. And he came to king Solomon, and wrought all his work.

Whoever this architect was, he created Solomon's Temple as a virtual replica of the Tyrian Temple of Melqart. He even added the two pillars outside the entrance. II Chronicles, *Chapter 3:17* states:

And he reared up the pillars before the temple, one on the right hand, and the other on the left; and called the name of that on the right hand Jachin, and the name of that on the left Boaz.

When the work of building the Temple was through, seven years later, Solomon made a point of filling it with objects that had already been dedicated to the Lord, as we read in *II Chronicles, Chapter 5:1*:

Thus all the work that Solomon made for the house of the LORD was finished: and Solomon brought in all the things that David his father had dedicated; and the silver, and the gold, and all the instruments, put he among the treasures of the house of God.

When dedicating the Temple, he made sacrifices of incalculable magnitude, to show his appreciation to God, as it says in *II Chronicles, Chapter 5:6*:

Also king Solomon, and all the congregation of Israel that were assembled unto him before the ark, sacrificed sheep and oxen, which could not be told nor numbered for multitude.

These were standard practices in the ancient world when commemorating a new temple. Such acts as building the temple with donated materials, filling it with religious treasures, and sacrificing animals upon a Temple's dedication were all believed to build up a powerful spiritual energy reserve within the temple, to turn it into a conduit for this power to be passed between the congregation and the gods they worshipped. So too was the placing of a special "cornerstone" in a temple's foundation. Solomon's Temple is said to have had a special cornerstone, which elsewhere in the Bible is used as a metaphor for Christ. Freemasons have used it as a symbol of the Philosopher's Stone. The Temple could be thought of as a living, growing organism, and the cornerstone as the seed at its root. In fact, Solomon's Temple had a number of vegetation motifs in its gold and brass work (representations of lilies, pomegranates, etc), which would tend to reinforce this notion.

The Temple became the central foundation of a new covenant between God and the Israelites, negotiated by Solomon after the Temple was built. Solomon asked for, and received, a new deal with God: as long as the people walked in the ways of God, there would never fail a son of David to sit upon the throne of Judah, and God would bless them abundantly all the days of their lives. If they sinned, they were to pray for forgiveness, in the direction of the Temple, in much the same way that Muslims now pray towards Mecca. *I Kings, Chapter 9:2-9:9* reads:

And the LORD said unto him, I have heard thy prayer and thy supplication, that thou hast made before me: I have hallowed this house, which thou hast built, to put my name there for ever; and mine eyes and mine heart shall be there perpetually. And if thou wilt walk before me, as David thy father walked, in integrity of heart, and in uprightness, to do according to all that I have commanded thee, and wilt keep my statutes and my judgments: Then I will establish the throne of thy kingdom upon Israel for ever, as I promised to David thy father, saying, There shall not fail thee a man upon the throne of Israel. But if ye shall at all turn from following me, ye or your children, and will not keep my commandments and my statutes which I have set before you, but go and serve other gods,

*and worship them: Then will I cut off Israel out of the land which I have
given them; and this house, which I have hallowed for my name, will I
cast out of my sight; and Israel shall be a proverb and a byword among
all people: And at this house, which is high, every one that passeth by it
shall be astonished, and shall hiss; and they shall say, Why hath the
LORD done thus unto this land, and to this house? And they shall
answer, Because they forsook the LORD their God, who brought forth
their fathers out of the land of Egypt, and have taken hold upon other
gods, and have worshipped them, and served them: therefore hath the
LORD brought upon them all this evil.*

In addition, even non-Israelite strangers could become involved in the
covenant, if they prayed towards the Temple. As we read in *II
Chronicles, Chapter 6:32 – 6:35*:

*Moreover concerning the stranger, which is not of thy people Israel, but
is come from a far country for thy great name's sake, and thy mighty
hand, and thy stretched out arm; if they come and pray in this house;
Then hear thou from the heavens, even from thy dwelling place, and do
according to all that the stranger calleth to thee for; that all people of the
earth may know thy name, and fear thee, as doth thy people Israel, and
may know that this house which I have built is called by thy name. If thy
people go out to war against their enemies by the way that thou shalt
send them, and they pray unto thee toward this city which thou hast
chosen, and the house which I have built for thy name; Then hear thou
from the heavens their prayer and their supplication, and maintain their
cause.*

The agreement even specifies that foreigners can appeal to Israel's god
and obtain victory in battle (provided that battle is not against Israel, of
course). One cannot help but think that Solomon interjected this
particular part into the agreement so that his friends in Tyre could enjoy
the benefits of the new covenant as well.

Chapter Sixteen:
King Solomon's Treasure

Just as the agreement had stipulated, after Solomon built the Temple, his kingdom's already voluminous wealth began to grow exponentially. As it states in *II Chronicles, Chapter 7:11*:

Thus Solomon finished the house of the LORD, and the king's house: and all that came into Solomon's heart to make in the house of the LORD, and in his own house, he prosperously effected.

One of the ways in which Solomon managed to increase his wealth was by having the subject nations in his empire pay him tributes. *I Kings, Chapter 4:21-24* tells us that Solomon's empire was quite large:

And Solomon reigned over all kingdoms from the river unto the land of the Philistines, and unto the border of Egypt: they brought presents, and served Solomon all the days of his life...

For he had dominion over all the region on this side the river, from Tiphsah even to Azzah, over all the kings on this side the river: and he had peace on all sides round about him.

I Kings, Chapter 9:20:22 also tells us how he forced the people of these subject nations to serve him as "bondmen": slaves. This is how the empire was maintained. It also specifies that Solomon exempted his own people from having to perform labor. It states:

And all the people that were left of the Amorites, Hittites, Perizzites, Hivites, and Jebusites, which were not of the children of Israel, Their children that were left after them in the land, whom the children of Israel also were not able utterly to destroy, upon those did Solomon levy a tribute of bondservice unto this day. But of the children of Israel did Solomon make no bondmen: but they were men of war, and his servants, and his princes, and his captains, and rulers of his chariots, and his horsemen.

In addition, Solomon even accepted gifts from foreign travelers who would come to hear him share his now world-renowned wisdom. Such was the case with the Queen of Sheba, who ruled another rich land, and came for an extended stay in Israel to test Solomon's wit. In *II Chronicles: Chapter 9:9* it says:

And she gave the king an hundred and twenty talents of gold, and of spices great abundance, and precious stones: neither was there any such spice as the queen of Sheba gave king Solomon.

More evidence of Solomon running his "wisdom racket" (in which he accepted gifts in exchange for dispersing advice) can be found in extra-biblical sources, such as those compiled in Louis Ginzberg's *Legends of the Jews, Volume IV*, where he quotes Jewish folk myths regarding the many riddle contests which Hiram and Solomon would have. Hiram would compose mind-bending riddles, which Solomon would inevitably crack, forcing Hiram to pay him a monetary tribute.

Through these various methods, and through international trade utilizing the ships and the shipping routes of the Tyrians, Solomon had a constant stream of wealth flowing into his country and constantly multiplying itself. As *I Kings, Chapter 10:14 – 10:29* describes it:

Now the weight of gold that came to Solomon in one year was six hundred threescore and six talents of gold. Beside that he had of the merchantmen, and of the traffick of the spice merchants, and of all the kings of Arabia, and of the governors of the country. And king Solomon made two hundred targets of beaten gold: six hundred shekels of gold went to one target. And he made three hundred shields of beaten gold; three pound of gold went to one shield: and the king put them in the house of the forest of Lebanon. Moreover the king made a great throne of ivory, and overlaid it with the best gold. The throne had six steps, and the top of the throne was round behind: and there were stays on either side on the place of the seat, and two lions stood beside the stays. And twelve lions stood there on the one side and on the other upon the six steps: there was not the like made in any kingdom. And all king Solomon's drinking vessels were of gold, and all the vessels of the house of the forest of Lebanon were of pure gold; none were of silver: it was nothing accounted of in the days of Solomon. For the king had at sea a navy of Tharshish with the navy of Hiram: once in three years came the navy of Tharshish, bringing gold, and silver, ivory, and apes, and peacocks. So king Solomon exceeded all the kings of the earth for riches and for wisdom. And all the earth sought to Solomon, to hear his wisdom, which God had put in his heart. And they brought every man his present, vessels of silver, and vessels of gold, and garments, and armour, and spices, horses, and mules, a rate year by year. And Solomon gathered together chariots and horsemen: and he had a thousand and four hundred chariots, and twelve thousand horsemen, whom he bestowed in the cities for chariots, and with the king at Jerusalem. And the king made silver to be in Jerusalem as stones, and cedars made he to be as the sycamore trees that are in the vale, for abundance. And Solomon had horses brought out of Egypt, and linen yarn: the king's merchants received the linen yarn at a price. And a chariot came up and went out of Egypt for six hundred shekels of silver, and an horse for an hundred and fifty: and so for all the kings of the Hittites, and for the kings of Syria, did they bring them out by their means.

But multiplying horses, wives, and gold unto oneself are three things specifically prohibited in the Hebrews scriptures for a king, who is supposed to remain humble and God-fearing. Solomon's wealth and decadent lifestyle was making him weak to the temptations of sin. Moreover, Solomon's many wives, including the daughter of the Pharaoh of Egypt, were turning his heart away from the one true God, and towards the abominable deities of the heathen. The scriptures tell us that his wives persuaded him to build temples to these other gods, including "Ashtoreth" and "Milcom", the equivalent of Tyre's Astarte and Melqart. We read in *I Kings, Chapter 11:1 – 11:10*:

But king Solomon loved many strange women, together with the daughter of Pharaoh, women of the Moabites, Ammonites, Edomites, Zidonians, and Hittites; Of the nations concerning which the LORD said unto the children of Israel, Ye shall not go in to them, neither shall they come in unto you: for surely they will turn away your heart after their gods: Solomon clave unto these in love. And he had seven hundred wives, princesses, and three hundred concubines: and his wives turned away his heart. For it came to pass, when Solomon was old, that his wives turned away his heart after other gods: and his heart was not perfect with the LORD his God, as was the heart of David his father. For Solomon went after Ashtoreth the goddess of the Zidonians, and after Milcom the abomination of the Ammonites. And Solomon did evil in the sight of the LORD, and went not fully after the LORD, as did David his father. Then did Solomon build an high place for Chemosh, the abomination of Moab, in the hill that is before Jerusalem, and for Molech, the abomination of the children of Ammon. And likewise did he for all his strange wives, which burnt incense and sacrificed unto their gods. And the LORD was angry with Solomon, because his heart was turned from the LORD God of Israel, which had appeared unto him twice, And had commanded him concerning this thing, that he should not go after other gods: but he kept not that which the LORD commanded.

Obviously, this constituted a breach in the contract that Solomon had with God, and it would cost him the kingdom. But God would not take it away during Solomon's lifetime. Honoring previous agreements with Solomon's ancestors, God allowed the kingdom to remain intact while Solomon lived, but rent it during the reign of his son Rehoboam. Always true to his contracts, God still allowed Solomon's descendant to keep the throne of Judah, Jerusalem, and rule over the tribe of Judah, again because of previous agreements, while the rest of the tribes were lost to his rival, Jeroboam. Thus were created the separate kingdoms of Judah and Israel, and from that time on, God was out to get them both, to punish them for the sins of Solomon. *I Kings, Chapter 11:12 – 11:13* tells us:

Wherefore the LORD said unto Solomon, Forasmuch as this is done of thee, and thou hast not kept my covenant and my statutes, which I have commanded thee, I will surely rend the kingdom from thee, and will give it to thy servant. Notwithstanding in thy days I will not do it for David thy father's sake: but I will rend it out of the hand of thy son. Howbeit I will not rend away all the kingdom; but will give one tribe to thy son for David my servant's sake, and for Jerusalem's sake which I have chosen.

Chapter Seventeen:
Solomon's Pact With the King of Demons

The classic book series, *The Legends of the Jews*, by Louis Ginzberg, which draws upon extra-Biblical Jewish, Arabic, and Christian sources, tells a very different account of Solomon's life. According to the story presented in *Volume IV* of this series, the main assistance which Solomon received in the building of the temple came not from Hiram of Tyre, but from demons. The text says that because of his wisdom, God gave Solomon to rule not only over his kingdom and empire, but over all beasts, and all spirits as well. It says that Solomon knew "the language of the birds", which is a form of cant described by alchemists as being all-powerful, able to command people, animals, and ethereal beings, and to alter physical reality. As the book explains:

Never has there lived a man privileged, like Solomon, to make the demons amenable to his will. God endowed him with the ability to turn the vicious power of demons into a power working to the advantage of men. He invented formulas of incantation by which diseases were alleviated, and others by which demons were exorcised so that they were banished forever. As his personal attendants he had spirits and demons whom he could send hither and thither on the instant. He could grow tropical plants in Palestine, because his ministering spirits secured water for him from India.

In this version of the story, when Solomon invited the Queen of Sheba to come visit him, he actually sent her a message demanding that she immediately come and pay homage to him, or else:

… I shall send out kings, legions, and riders against thee. Thou askest, who are these kings, legions, and riders of King Solomon? The beasts of the field are my kings, the birds my riders, the demons, spirit, and shades of the night my legions. The demons will throttle you in your beds at night, while the beasts will slay you in the field, and the birds will consume your flesh.

So when it came time for Solomon's most ambitious project, the building of the Temple, it was natural that Solomon would turn to the demonic realm for help, according to this account. This was actually not terribly unusual for the time. In an ancient world where it was quite normal to make contracts with spirits in order to obtain one's desires, a demon's assistance in building something was one of the most common requests. Architecture was believed to be one of their areas of expertise, as was the forging of metals, since demons ruled over the subterranean caverns in which these substances were found. But in this story, for the building of the very House of God, Solomon would enlist the help of the greatest demon of all, Asmodeus, whom he compelled to obey him by the use of a magical signet ring. Louis Ginzberg tells us:

The demons were of greatest service to Solomon during the erection of the Temple. It came about in this wise: When Solomon began the building of the Temple, it once happened that a malicious spirit snatched away the money and the food of one of the king's favorite pages. This occurred several times, and Solomon was not able to lay hold on the malefactor. The king besought God fervently to deliver the wicked spirit into his hands. His prayer was granted. The archangel Michael appeared to him, and gave him a small ring having a seal consisting of an engraved stone, and he said to him: 'Take, O Solomon, king, son of David, the gift which the Lord God, the highest Zebaot, hath sent unto thee. With it thou shalt lock up all the demons of the earth, male and female; and with their help thou shalt build up Jerusalem. But thou must wear this seal of God; and this engraving of the seal of the ring sent thee is a Pentalpha.'

The seal of Solomon's ring, the "pentalpha", is just another word for the pentagram. It is so called because, if you look at a pentagram, you will notice that you can actually break it down into three triangles, and also three letters "A", or the Greek "alpha." This is the true "Seal of Solomon", and he used it as all magicians have traditionally used it since then: to imprison demonic spirits, and to bind them to their will. The pentagram is called the "Endless Knot", and was first used by the ancient Sumerians as a sign which meant "shackle" or "prison." It was even used as the City Seal of Jerusalem, according to an article called "the pentagram" on the website of the Masonic Grand Lodge of British Columbia and Yukon, which adds:

Roman Emperor Constantine I, after his defeat of Maxentius and the issuance of the Edict of Milan in 312CE, ascribed his success to his conversion to Christianity and incorporated the pentagram, one point down, into his seal and amulet.

The six-pointed star is more widely referred to nowadays as the "Seal of Solomon", and also as the "Star of David." But anciently, both symbols were used for similar purposes, and both were called by each of those names. However, it was most definitely the pentagram which was featured on Solomon's magical ring. As Ginzberg relates:

Armed with it, Solomon called up all the demons before him, and he asked of each in turn his or her name, as well as the name of the star or constellation or zodiacal sign and of the particular angel to the influence of which each is subject. One after another the spirits were vanquished, and compelled by Solomon to aid in the construction of the Temple.

The manner in which Asmodeus became involved in the building of the Temple occurred when Solomon sought the help of a magical worm called the "shamir", which was capable of cutting stone. *Legends of the Jews* reads:

While Solomon was occupied with the Temple, he had great difficulty in devising ways of fitting the stone from the quarry into the building, for the Torah explicitly prohibits the use of iron tools in erecting an altar. The scholars told him that Moses had used the shamir, the stone that splits rocks, to engrave the names of the tribes on the precious stones of the ephod worn by the high priest. Solomon's demons could give him no information as to where the shamir could be found. They surmised, however, that Asmodeus, king of demons, was in possession of the secret, and they told Solomon the name of the mountain on which Asmodeus dwelt, and described also his manner of life. On this mountain there was a well from which Asmodeus obtained his drinking water. He closed it up daily with a large rock, and sealed it before going to heaven, whither he went every day, to take part in the discussions in the heavenly academy. Thence he would descend again to earth in order to be present, though invisible, at the debates in the earthly houses of learning. Then, after investigating the seal on the well to ascertain if it had been tampered with, he drank of the water.

Clearly, Asmodeus, as king of the demons, was also seen as one of the keepers of heavenly wisdom. This is made apparent by the fact that he is presented as participating in intellectual debates at the "heavenly academy", and oversees those which take place at schools on Earth. This accords with the ancient interpretation of the word "demon", which literally translates as "wise one."

But as wise as Asmodeus was, Solomon managed to pull one over on him. He had the demon's drinking well filled with wine instead of water. Once he was all good and drunk, Asmodeus was easily captured, and compelled to spill the beans regarding the shamir worm. The text continues:

Asmodeus told Solomon that the shamir was given by God to the Angel of the Sea, and that Angel entrusted none with the shamir except the moor-hen, which had taken an oath to watch the shamir carefully. The moor-hen takes the shamir with her to mountains which are not inhabited by men, splits them by means of the shamir, and injects seeds, which grow and cover the naked rocks, and then they can be inhabited. Solomon sent one of his servants to seek the nest of the bird and lay a piece of glass over it. When the moor-hen came and could not reach her young, she flew away and fetched the shamir and placed it on the glass. Then the man shouted, and so terrified the bird that she dropped the shamir and flew away. By this means the man obtained possession of the coveted shamir, and bore it to Solomon. But the moor-hen was so distressed at having broken her oath to the Angel of the Sea that she committed suicide.

Taking Asmodeus captive proved to be very helpful for Solomon, not only because he led the king's men to the shamir, but also because he became, in many ways, the chief architect of the Temple, at least according to the legends provided by Ginzberg. In this version of events, King Hiram of Tyre appears to play only a minor role in the building of the Temple, and the other Hirams, including the architect Hiram, are not mentioned at all. Instead, Asmodeus is playing the role of the architect Hiram.

Using the king of demons to build the Temple proved to be not only helpful to Solomon, but harmful as well. The spirit was too crafty for Solomon, and managed to trick him into giving up the source of his power. As *Legends of the Jews* states:

Although Asmodeus was captured only for the purpose of getting the shamir, Solomon nevertheless kept him after the completion of the Temple. One day the king told Asmodeus that he did not understand wherein the greatness of the demons lay, if their king could be kept in bonds by a mortal. Asmodeus replied, that if Solomon would remove his chains and lend him the magic ring, he would prove his own greatness. Solomon agreed. The demon stood before him with one wing touching heaven and the other reaching to the earth. Snatching up Solomon, who had parted with his protecting ring, he flung him four hundred parasangs away from Jerusalem, and then palmed himself off as the king.

Solomon was carried off so far away from Jerusalem that nobody recognized who he was. Separated from his ring, and all other accoutrements of power, Solomon was forced to wander about as a miserly beggar, desperately trying to convince everyone was he was the famous, wise, and wealthy King Solomon. But everyone who heard this thought he was a madman, for Solomon was thought to still be ruling with great pomp from Jerusalem. You see, Asmodeus had transformed himself into the king's likeness, and was ruling in his stead, with none being any the wiser. Meanwhile, Solomon took up residence with the king of the Ammonites (in modern Egypt), whom he served as chief cook. Solomon ended up falling in love with the king's daughter, and this turned out to be the key to regaining his throne. As Ginzberg explains:

At the end of that time, God took mercy upon him for the sake of his father David, and for the sake of the pious princess Naamah, the daughter of the Ammonite king, destined by God to be the ancestress of the Messiah. The time was approaching when she was to become the wife of Solomon and reign as queen in Jerusalem. God therefore led the royal wanderer to the capital city of Ammon. Solomon took service as an underling with the cook in the royal household, and he proved himself so proficient in the culinary art that the king of Ammon raised him to the post of chief cook. Thus he came under the notice of the king's daughter Naamah, who fell in love with her father's cook. In vain her parents endeavored to persuade her to choose a husband befitting her rank. Not even the king's threat to have her and her beloved executed availed to turn her thoughts away from Solomon. The Ammonite king had the lovers taken to a barren desert, in the hope that they would die of starvation there. Solomon and his wife wandered through the desert until they came to a city situated by the sea-shore. They purchased a fish to stave off death. When Naamah prepared the fish, she found in its belly the magic ring belonging to her husband, which he had given to Asmodeus, and which, thrown into the sea by the demon, had been swallowed by a fish. Solomon recognized his ring, put it on his finger, and in the twinkling of an eye he transported himself to Jerusalem. Asmodeus, who had been posing as King Solomon during the three years, he drove out, and himself ascended the throne again.

It seems clear that this Asmodeus figure bears many parallels and possible connections to the figure of Baphomet. For one thing, they are both demons, and both associated with wisdom, Asmodeus being responsible for overseeing the academic institutions of both Heaven and Earth. Masonic author Albert Pike referred to the Temple of Solomon as a "Temple builded by Wisdom." Asmodeus is here being credited with building that Temple, the foundation of which the Knights Templar lived on top of, and excavated underneath looking for treasure, perhaps finding there the head of Baphomet, and/or other religious artifacts. Indeed, it was this Temple which they named their organization after. Could Asmodeus have left something behind when he was building the Temple – something which the Templars later used to contact him, under the name of "Baphomet"?

In addition to being described as a skull or a head, Baphomet was also said to be a demonic creature with a goat's head, and a human body, with both male and female sexual organs. In this guise, Baphomet has been depicted (most memorably by nineteenth-century occultist Eliphas Levi) as seated upon a throne, with one arm pointing up towards the heavens, and the other down below the Earth, embodying the concept of the unity of opposites that Baphomet represents. How can we resist comparison, then, when Asmodeus strikes the exact same pose right before he assumes the likeness of Solomon? Recall what the text said:

The demon stood before him <u>with one wing touching heaven and the other reaching to the earth</u>. Snatching up Solomon, who had parted with his protecting ring, he flung him four hundred parasangs away from Jerusalem, and then palmed himself off as the king.

"Asmodeus" contains the root word "As", or "Az", that we also find in "Azoth", another word for the alchemical concept that Baphomet symbolizes, as well as the demon "Azazel", the name of the Scapegoat traditionally sacrificed by the Levite priests of Israel on Yom Kippur. It is also the name of a demon who, according to Judeo-Christian apocryphal legends, was shackled to a mountain forever as punishment for having taught forbidden wisdom to mankind. This very myth is referenced in the story of Solomon in *Legends of the Jews*, where "Azazel" is split into two characters, "Azza" and "Azzael." Nevertheless, it is clear that this is a reference to the same figure. It says:

As the spirits were subservient to [Solomon], so also the animals. He had an eagle upon whose back he was transported to the desert and back again in one day, to build there the city called Tadmor in the Bible. This city must not be confounded with the later Syrian city of Palmyra, also called Tadmor. It was situated near the 'mountains of darkness,' the trysting-place of the spirits and demons. Thither the eagle would carry Solomon in the twinkling of an eye, and Solomon would drop a paper inscribed with a verse among the spirits, to ward off evil from himself. Then the eagle would reconnoitre the mountains of darkness, until he had spied out the spot in which the fallen angels 'Azza and 'Azzael lie chained with iron fetters, a spot which no one, not even a bird, may visit. When the eagle found the place, he would take Solomon under his left wing, and fly to the two angels. Through the power of the ring having the Holy Name graven upon it, which Solomon put into the eagle's mouth, 'Azza and 'Azzael were forced to reveal the heavenly mysteries to the king.

So Azazel is revealed in this story to be yet another purported source of some of Solomon's wisdom. Azazel seems to equate to the figure of Asmodeus, who also is the same figure later called Azoth by the alchemists, and Baphomet by the Templars.

Chapter Eighteen:
The Universal Agent

The Baphometic and alchemical concept of the balance of opposites is represented in Solomon's Temple with the two pillars that were placed outside of the entrance. As I have mentioned, these were replicas of the ones that stood outside of the Temple of Melqart on Tyre, which in turn were meant to represent the Pillars of Hercules. At Solomon's Temple they were named "Jachin", which means "He shall establish", and "Boaz", which means "It is in strength." These pillars came to be a powerful symbol for occultists and Freemasons, to whom they now represent the opposites of light and dark, male and female, etc. Jachin is sometimes shown as white in color, with Boaz as its opposite, black. The two pillars are represented at the entrance of each Masonic lodge, which is always (when possible) facing East. Masonic writer Albert Pike analyzes the meaning of the names of the pillars in *Morals and Dogma*:

The word Jachin, in Hebrew... was probably pronounced Ya-kayan, and meant, as a verbal noun, He that strengthens; and thence, firm, stable, upright.

The word Boaz is Baaz ... [and it] means Strong, Strength, Power, Might, Refuge, Source of Strength, a Fort. The prefix means 'with' or 'in,' and gives the word the force of the Latin gerund, roborando - Strengthening.

The former word also means he will establish, or plant in an erect position - from the verb Kun, he stood erect. It probably meant Active and Vivifying Energy and Force; and Boaz, Stability, Permanence, in the passive sense.

Elsewhere, Pike states that Jachin and Boaz together represent "the unlimited Power and Splendor of Perfection of the Deity."

Baphomet too, according to Pike, represents "unlimited power." Pike has this to say about Baphomet in *Morals and Dogma*, linking him to the alchemical "Universal Agent" called the "Azoth" that supposedly could be used to create the Philosopher's Stone, or to turn lead into gold:

There is in nature one most potent force, by means where of a single man, who could possess himself of it, and should know how to direct it, could revolutionize and change the face of the world.

This force was known to the ancients. It is a universal agent, whose supreme law is equilibrium, and whereby, if science can but learn how to control it, it will be possible to change the order of the seasons, to produce in night the phenomena of day, to send a thought in an instant round the world, to heal or to slay at a distance, to give our words universal success, and make them reverberate everywhere.

This agent, partially revealed by the blind guesses of Mesmer, is precisely what the Adepts of the Middle Ages called the elementary matter of the great work. The Gnostics held that it composed the igneous body of the Holy Spirit; and it was adored in the secret rites of the Sabbat or the Temple, under the hieroglyphic figure of Baphomet or the hermaphroditic goat of Mendes.

So this is what Baphomet was: a "universal agent", created through the unity of opposing forces of nature, which composes a new force, powerful enough to alter physical reality, from the atomic level upward. It is the very same Philosopher's Stone of the alchemists, capable of turning dross matter into gold. The possession of the secret of this force would presumably place its possessors amongst the most powerful people in the world. It seems probable that this is the wisdom that Solomon possessed, which enabled him not only to control animals and spirits (as *The Legends of the Jews* suggests), but also to become fabulously wealthy. Louis Ginzberg tells us that when Solomon was granted a wish by God, he chose wisdom not because he was uninterested in money or power, but because he was already smart enough to know that "wisdom once in his possession, all else would come of itself." Solomon's wisdom led him to utilize economic principles that were little understood at the time, and not widely used. It also seems likely that he learned more specifics about managing an economy from Hiram of Tyre.

It further seems just as likely that the keys to finding and utilizing this "universal agent" were encoded into the architecture of Solomon's "temple builded by Wisdom", as Masonic legends explicitly state they were. Indeed, the practice of Freemasonry largely involves the study of sacred geometric principles believed to have been used in the building of Solomon's Temple. Masonic legend also suggests that the Freemasons possess these secrets because they were discovered by the Knights Templar while excavating beneath the Temple Mount.

Chapter Nineteen:
The Plot to Rebuild the Temple

But would the Templars necessarily have known what to look for under the Temple Mount, or have understood it when they found it? They could have, if information regarding this had been passed down hereditarily from biblical times onward. This was the premise of the bestselling 1980s book *Holy Blood, Holy Grail*, by Michael Baigent, Richard Leigh, and Henry Lincoln. The book alleged that the founders of the Templars, including the famous Godfroi de Bouillon and Hughes de Payen, were descendants of a royal bloodline which traced its roots back to Jesus Christ and thus, ultimately, to King Solomon. Modern scions of this bloodline were quoted in *Holy Blood, Holy Grail* as claiming to know the whereabouts of the Ark of the Covenant, and numerous other biblical secrets, which were said to have been passed down from generation to generation from the Bible characters themselves.

If the Templars truly were the descendants of biblical figures, they probably also had in their veins the blood of the Levite priests. It would seem clear that, bloodline or no, the Templars saw themselves as fulfilling the role that the Levites once did. The Templars too were priests, and performed the duties of banking for the community, as the Levites did. But more importantly, they were performing the Levites' chief function of overseeing the activities of the Temple – even if it was, at the time, only the foundation of the building that remained. Also in this context, we should note the Templars' devotion to John the Baptist, who was a direct descendant of the first Levite High Priest, Aaron.

But if the Templars did have Jewish genes, Levite genes were likely among them. Since ten tribes of Israel were destroyed by the Babylonian captivity, only three remained: those of Judah, Benjamin, and Levi (which, although not counted as a "tribe" biblically, technically were). These then became interspersed with each other so much in Israel that they were virtually indistinguishable in many ways. So by the time of the Templars, chances were good that if you were of Jewish ancestry at all, it probably included the lines of both Judah and Levi.

In this regard, there is an interesting detail to note: the Templars were obviously highly involved in creating the Latin Kingdom of Jerusalem after the capture of the city during the First Crusade – so much so that one of the Templar founders, Godfroi de Bouillon, was offered the crown of the new kingdom. He declined the title, choosing instead to call himself "Defender of the Holy Sepulcher", but he was succeeded by his brother Baudouin, who accepted the title to become King Baldwin I. Strangely, both men are reported to have converted to Judaism upon taking their titles. Perhaps it was their known association with Judaism and Jewish bloodlines which persuaded the Pope to grant the Templars the right to practice usury.

Albert Pike argues in *Morals and Dogma* that the Templars not only discovered the secrets of the Temple of Solomon, but that they actively wanted to *rebuild* the Temple. This, he says, was all part of their larger plot to take over the world through the power of money. He also alleges that they colluded with the Byzantine Church in this plot, because they too shared the dream of rebuilding Solomon's Temple, as part of their goal of supplanting the Roman Church. As Pike explains it:

In 1118, nine Knights Crusaders in the East, among whom were Geoffroi de Saint-Omer and Hugues de Payens, consecrated themselves to religion, and took an oath between the hands of the Patriarch of Constantinople, a See always secretly or openly hostile to that of Rome from the time of Photius. The avowed object of the Templars was to protect the Christians who came to visit the Holy Places: their secret object was the re-building of the Temple of Solomon...

This re-building, formally predicted by the Judaizing Mystics of the earlier ages, had become the secret dream of the Patriarchs of the Orient. The Temple of Solomon, re-built and consecrated to the Catholic worship would become, in effect, the Metropolis of the Universe; the East would prevail over the West, and the Patriarchs of Constantinople would possess themselves of the Papal power.

However, Pike tells us that the Templars were not exactly loyal to the Eastern Church, but more so to the Gnostic doctrines taught by John the Baptist. Pike even claims that the Templar leader Hughes de Payens was initiated into a secret Johannite church led by supposed direct linear successors of John's priesthood. In fact, Pike states that de Payens himself was made a successor of that priesthood. Pike writes:

The secret thought of Hugues de Payens, in founding his Order, was not exactly to serve the ambition of the Patriarchs of Constantinople. There existed at that period in the East a Sect of Johannite Christians, who claimed to be the only true Initiates into the real mysteries of the religion of the Saviour...

...The Johannites ascribed to Saint John the foundation of their Secret

Church, and the Grand Pontiffs of the Sect assumed the title of Christos, Anointed, or Consecrated, and claimed to have succeeded one another from Saint John by an uninterrupted succession of pontifical powers. He who, at the period of the foundation of the Order of the Temple, claimed these imaginary prerogatives, was named THEOCLET; he knew HUGUES DE PAYENS, he initiated him into the Mysteries and hopes of his pretended church, he seduced him by the notions of Sovereign Priesthood and Supreme royalty, and finally designated him as his successor.

Thus, one could say that the Baphometic wisdom believed to be possessed by John the Baptist (symbolized by the image of his severed head or skull), along with the priestly prerogatives that John was entitled to as the lead descendant of the High Priest Aaron, were legitimately bestowed upon another likely descendant of Aaron, Hughes de Payens. Armed with this, the Templars may have felt that they already possessed more real power than any institution on Earth. Says Pike:

To acquire influence and wealth, then to intrigue, and at need to fight, to establish the Johannite or Gnostic and Kabalistic dogma, were the object and means proposed to the initiated Brethren. The Papacy and the rival monarchies, they said to them, are sold and bought in these days, become corrupt, and to-morrow, perhaps, will destroy each other. All that will become the heritage of the Temple: the World will soon come to us for its Sovereigns and Pontiffs. We shall constitute the equilibrium of the Universe, and be rulers over the Masters of the World...

...Their watchword was, to become wealthy, in order to buy the world.

Pike then goes on to describe how their arrogant pretensions led to the persecution and downfall of the Templar Order. But, he says, before the last Grand Master, Jacques de Molay, was consigned to the flames for heresy and witchcraft, he arranged for the work of the Templars to be carried on after his death by a new institution: Freemasonry. As he explains it:

The end of the drama is well known, and how Jacques de Molai and his fellows perished in the flames. But before his execution, the Chief of the doomed Order organized and instituted what afterward came to be called the Occult, Hermetic, or Scottish Masonry. In the gloom of his prison, the Grand Master created four Metropolitan Lodges, at Naples for the East, at Edinburg for the West, at Stockholm for the North, and at Paris for the South.

The fact that Albert Pike connects the Templars directly to the Byzantine church brings to mind an interesting possibility that I would like to present. It involved the well-known Templar standard, or battle flag, which showed their trademark red equilateral cross on a black and white chequered field.

Chapter Twenty:
The Beautiful One

I have previously mentioned that the Templars picked up use of the chequer pattern from their contacts in the East, possibly from Islamic sources, but more likely from the Byzantines. Like Jachin and Boaz, this pattern represented to the Templars their Baphometic concept of the unity of opposites. They also held, as Freemasons do today, that the floor of Solomon's Temple was covered with black and white chequered tiles. All of these concepts, and that of the Baphomet itself, were symbolized by the Templar flag, which they actually had a name for. They called it "Beaussant", which means "the beautiful one."

Clearly there is a similarity between this word, "beaussant", and the root word "Byzant" in Byzantine. Of course, "Byzantium" was not called that during its time. It was only called that later on by seventeenth century scholars. The origin of the name is said to have come from the mythical (pre-Constantine) founder of the area who supposedly was named "Byzas." But this explanation is not widely accepted. Nobody really knows why it was called that. But the coins which Constantine had minted to pay for the construction of Constantinople (out of the gold looted from pagan Roman temples) were called "besants", and they continued to be the currency of the empire afterwards. The word "Byzantine" is now used as an adjective to describe any form of complex pattern, and this comes from the mosaic nature of Byzantine art. The chequer pattern is commonly used is Byzantine art, the chequer pattern being one of the most commonly used. The Templars may have picked up use of it when they passed through Constantinople during the First Crusade, just as they patterned the design of their monasteries after the domed architecture of Byzantium, most especially, the Hagia Sophia (the Church of the Holy Wisdom).

This lends further credence to the possibility that the words "beaussant" and "Byzant" may be related. And too, one might consider a common origin in the word "Boaz", which Albert Pike tells us was also pronounced "Baaz."

Later on in history, we find that many of the early Freemasons or "proto-Masons" became engaged as privateers, or "pirates", sailing the high seas in search of plunder. They too had a battle flag that represented the Baphomet. It was a black field upon which was featured the famous Templar and Masonic symbol of the skull and crossbones. And they had a cute name for it too: "the Jolly Roger." The origin of this is mysterious, but it is possible that "Roger" refers in code to the Hebrew word for "head", which is "rosh."

The fact that Baphomet, or the head of John the Baptist, would be represented on these two flags brings to mind other interesting possible linguistic connections. A flag is sometimes called a "jack", as in the "Union Jack" of Britain. Of course, "Jack" is also a popular nickname for a person named "John", although it is sometimes an anglicized version of the French name "Jacques." These connections stem from the common origin of all of these names in Hebrew. Also related are "James", "Jacob", and "Jachin." The names "James" and "Jacob" were still considered interchangeable in Britain in the 1600s, when supporters of the Stuart kings James I and II were called "Jacobites."

But "John", or "Johannes", is also related anciently to "Oannes", the name of a Babylonian deity who was remembered for having taught divine wisdom to mankind. This name, in turn, is related to the name of the Roman deity "Janus", who, as with some descriptions of the Baphomet head, had two faces, and was recalled by the Romans as having invented the concept of money. "Jnana" means "wisdom" in Hindi. "Sion", a name for the Temple Mount in Jerusalem, is also the Welsh way of saying "John." Furthermore, we should consider the Persian word "djinn" (pronounced "jin"), which means "genius" or "demon." Finally, it should be noted that "jack" is also a term that has been used to refer to ghosts or demons, as well as being a slang term for money. All of these concepts are linked with that of the Baphomet.

But if this is not enough to link John to the concept of Baphomet, the Masons make it explicit with their iconographic depiction of him posing in the now "Baphometic" stance, with one hand pointing up to Heaven, and the other pointing down to the Earth.

Chapter Twenty-One:
Triskadekaphilia

Returning to the subject of the Jolly Roger, there was one more notable detail that appeared on the flag, beneath the skull and crossbones. It was the number "13", written in Arabic numerals, with no explanation given.

The origins of this must lie with the associations between the Templars and the number thirteen, which seem to have been applied to them, although perhaps only after the fact, through legend, because their arrest and persecution by the king of France began on Friday the Thirteenth of October, in 1307. In addition, I discussed previously the fact that the Templars apparently had possession of a golden head (which may have been one of their auxiliary Baphomet heads) labeled "Caput 58 M", with the "M" written as the astrological symbol for Virgo. I mentioned that this could be a code for 13, because the digits 5 and 8 add up to 13. Also, "M" is the thirteenth letter of not only our own alphabet, but many others, including the Hebrew. In addition, I mentioned what appears to be a Knights Templar spin-off group called the Priory of Sion, which observes the use of a thirteen-house zodiac system. In this system, Virgo may have been considered the "thirteenth house." It is possible that this same zodiac system was used by the Knights Templar. Either way, it is evidence that the number 13 was important to the Templars, and that they associated it with the head of Baphomet. This then may be the origin of the number thirteen beneath the skull and crossbones on the Jolly Roger flag.

In my previous book, *The Merovingian Mythos and the Mystery of Rennes-le-Chateau*, I discussed the rather voluminous evidence that the Priory of Sion certainly considered the number thirteen to be important. I even demonstrated how their use of a membership ranking system based on multiples of thirteen contained a hidden lunar calendar, based on lunar years of 364 days. I also discussed the fact that a 52-piece deck of playing cards contains a hidden lunar calendar as well. This, I stated, was particularly interesting given the historical evidence indicating that the Knights Templar may have played a role in bringing playing cards to the West from Eastern sources, and also may have helped to modify them into the form in which we see them today. Incidentally, playing cards directly influenced the development of the Tarot deck, and in modern tarot decks (such as the standard one developed by Arthur Edward Waite, a Freemason), the card labeled "XIII" is "Death." Also, Masonic lodges usually meet every full moon, which means there are thirteen of these lunar meetings every year.

Other possible connections with the number thirteen that may have been important to the Templars include the fact that the tribe of Levi was at one time the thirteenth tribe of Israel, but at the same time considered not a tribe, with special rights restrictions, and special duties. As I have explained, the Levites did not have a territory of their own, but their domains were scattered about the territories of the other tribes. In a way, the activities of the Templars reflected this, in that they did not have any particular land assigned to them, but possessed a right of sovereignty which allowed them to be a law unto themselves. Like the Templars, the Levites were not allowed to own property, but lived well by taking donations from the people they served. So if the Templars were copying the Levites in some symbolic way, they may have taken on the number 13 as a symbol for that reason.

Another possible connection deals with King Solomon who, as I said previously, spent thirteen years building his royal palace, immediately after building the Temple. *The Book of Kings* actually states that the pillars of Jachin and Boaz were on the outside of *this* building, not outside the entrance to the actual Temple. The Templars are believed to have spelunked in the caves underneath the palace as well. So perhaps the Templar "13" is a reference to this building. But perhaps a stronger connection between 13 and Solomon (and the concept of the Baphomet) is hinted at with this quote from *The Legends of the Jews*:

The 'forty-nine gates of wisdom' were open to Solomon as they had been to Moses...

We should note too, I suppose, that Constantine, another possible possessor of the Baphomet head at one time, was called the "thirteenth apostle."

However, I think the most important connections are those between the skull and crossbones, the number 13, and alchemy. The skull and crossbones, or sometimes just a skull, is called a "death's head" in occult parlance, and it has been used by alchemists at least since the Middle Ages to symbolize the "nigrido", the primary stage in the alchemical process, when the initial substance which one is attempting to transform (usually, into gold), is broken down into its original atomic components – called "prima material" ("first matter") in alchemy. The idea is that an object or substance must be utterly destroyed and disintegrated, down to the atomic level, before it can be translated into something else. Thus, this stage of the process is identified with "death", while the creation of the new substance is compared with "rebirth." A good way of picturing this would be to think of the way in which people and objects are "beamed" from one place to another on the TV show *Star Trek*. The technology used on that show is all based upon these ancient alchemical ideas. Another prefect example is the replicator machine used on *Star Trek*, which essentially can make any thing or substance seemingly out of nothing, using pure energy as the "prima materia."

Interestingly, according to some, there are exactly thirteen stages in the alchemical process. These, according to legend, are written upon the "Emerald Tablet of Hermes", a green stone that supposedly fell from Heaven. The study of alchemy was greatly advanced in Hellenized Egypt, and that is where the myth of the Greek god Hermes invention of alchemy developed. Hermes would seem to be yet another figure upon whom the character of Baphomet was based. This is made obvious, if nothing else, by the fact that Hermes is often portrayed in statues and drawings pointing one hand up, and the other down. Also, Hermes was traditionally viewed as one of the satyrs, which were half-man, half-goat creatures from Greek mythology, just as Baphomet was seen as half-human and half-goat. Then consider the fact that Hermes was known for teaching alchemical wisdom to mankind, and his eternal symbol was the caduceus: a staff with two serpents entwined upon it (or sometimes one). The Eliphas Levi depiction of Baphomet shows him with a double-serpent caduceus formed around the base of his penis. Finally, I note that Baphomet is a "hermaphrodite", both male and female, a word that comes from the name "Hermes", and that of the Greek goddess "Aphrodite." Mark Amaru Pinkham writes in *Guardians of the Holy Grail: The Knights Templar, John the Baptist, and the Water of Life,* that:

...13 was also very important for the alchemical process because it denoted the number of stages in the alchemical process leading to death and rebirth. Legend has it that these 13 stages were inscribed by the sage Thoth-Hermes as 13 precepts on a tablet called the Emerald Tablet that was made of solid emerald; thus, the stages leading to the creation of the Philosopher's Stone were themselves inscribed on a version of the Philosopher's Stone. These 13 precepts became the foundation of Egyptian alchemy, and they were later inculcated within the Islamic Universities of Constantinople and Seville...

Of course, other sources say that there are ten, or sometimes seven, stages of alchemy denoted by the Emerald Tablet, but who's counting. Pinkham also makes the following observations:

Three very important 'alchemical' numbers eventually occurred to the alchemists from observing the cycles of Venus. The first number was eight, which is the number of [Earth] years it takes for Venus' cycle to elapse; the second number was five, the number of times the planet becomes the Morning and Evening Stars during the cycle; and the third was thirteen, the number of times Venus revolved around the sun during the span of eight years. Of these numbers, the Arabic number 8 was adopted by alchemists as their definitive symbol for polarity union and the infinite state of immortality in engenders. The number 8 symbolized polarity union as two united circles, and also revealed that alchemy was the union of two circular 'worlds', Heaven and Earth. The number and symbol 8 became so important to the early alchemists that they made it the sacred number of their eternal patron, the Egyptian Thoth-Hermes.

Thus the "58" in "Caput 58M" could be a reference to all three of these numbers: 5, 8, and 13, and thus, the heavenly cycles of Venus. It is also noteworthy that the Templars are specifically remembered not for being arrested on "October the thirteenth" so much as on "Friday the thirteenth." Friday was named after "Freya", the Norse name for Venus.

Furthermore, 5, 8, and 13 are among the first numbers found in the "Fibonacci sequence. This is a sequence of numbers which represents the growth pattern of all living things in nature: of the embryo as it becomes a fetus, then a baby, then a child, then an adult, or of a seed that becomes a seedling, then a plant. This contains the Fibonacci sequence of 2, 3, 5, 8, and 13. The Fibonacci sequence defines itself geometrically in things like the "golden spiral", the "golden mean proportion", and the pentagram (see figures 25 and 26). These are shapes found everywhere in nature, as they are visual representations of the mathematical sequences at work in creation. Long ago, ancient astronomers noticed that the movements of Venus contain Fibonacci numbers and golden mean geometry, yet more reasons why they held the goddess Venus to be sacred. No wonder, then, that the Fibonacci sequence and golden geometry are important to the studies of sacred geometry and alchemy.

You could even say that the Fibonacci sequence is what mathematically unifies the study of alchemy and the study of sacred geometry. Golden Mean geometry and Fibonacci numbers were used in the building of the pyramids, and, it is rumored, Solomon's Temple. Undoubtedly they could be found in the Hagia Sophia. Later on from about 1100, medieval stonemasons hired by the Knights Templar used the same principles, utilized in a different way, to create the magnificent the Gothic cathedrals of Europe. Because they are made from the numbers and geometry of nature, these buildings symbolically acted as living organisms, a theme emphasized ever more so by the common use of floral, agricultural, and other plant motifs for decoration.

But the number 13 plays some specific roles in the geometry of nature that are very interesting. One is that there are thirteen geometric solids in the third dimension, as classified by the Greek philosopher and mathematician, Archimedes. The other is that thirteen spheres, when placed together, make the most tightly compact arrangement of spheres mathematically allowable. When arranged this way, they form a three-dimensional representation of a hexagon. This brings to mind the thirteen stars arranged in the form of a larger, six-pointed star, which we find above the head of the eagle on the front piece to the Great Seal of the United States. In each of these arrangements, the thirteenth piece is the hidden element which unifies and perfects the whole – like the Philosopher's Stone of the alchemists. This is the same symbolism found on the reverse of the Great Seal, signified by the All-Seeing Eye which completes the pyramid. In his book *A Beginner's Guide to Constructing the Universe*, Michael S. Schneider illustrates how hexagonal geometry can be applied to the entire front side on the Great Seal (see figure 30). Furthermore, the hexagram is implied on the reverse of the Seal as well, formed when you connect the All-Seeing Eye with the letters "M", "A", "S", "O", and "N", to spell "mason."

This brings me to another interesting observation that Michael Schneider made in his book regarding the number 13:

Twelve is related to thirteen, the notorious but misunderstood number of superstition. While twelve is a solar number, thirteen is lunar, as the twelve months of a solar year contain nearly thirteen lunations. The relationship is more obvious when we look geometrically. Each of the methods for constructing a dodecagon results in twelve equally spaced points around a thirteenth on at the center. Twelve points occur at the crossings of a hexagram star around the thirteenth at their center...

Less well-known is the existence of a twelve-around-one pattern in the government of the United States, the founders of which were Freemasons. Seeking to establish a utopian society in the ancient tradition, they gave the government a classic twelvefold structure-function-order. In every way possible they incorporated zodiacal symbolism. George Washington kept a circle of twelve generals around him to fight for the thirteen colonies. The symbolism of thirteen stars and thirteen stripes on their flag, thirteen letters in their motto, 'E Pluribus Unum' ('From many, one'), and thirteen buttons on the sailor's uniform accented their intent. The number of colonies was not accidental but a hidden reference to an ancient teaching.

To this I would add that the flag of the Confederate States of America (which had many Freemasons, including Albert Pike, heading its cause) bore thirteen stars as well. This is because there were really thirteen secessionist states in the Confederacy, even though history books often cite only 11. (The states of Kentucky and Missouri each had mini-civil wars within themselves, with each having both a Unionist government, and a break-away Confederate government.) At any rate, it seems that, even if the number 13 is not an especially "Masonic" number per se, it was a sacred number, the associations of which the Masonic founders of the United States were certainly familiar with. Could this be the meaning of the use of 13 by the USA's founders: that it signifies both the unifying principle, and the principle of creation, that is at once the Philosopher's Stone of the alchemists, and the Templar concept of Baphomet?

When placed on the US one dollar bill, this representation of the Baphomet, made by the repeated use of the number thirteen, takes on a greater significance pertaining to alchemical nature of fiat currency. Baphomet was, to the Templars, the key to applied alchemy – both economically and otherwise. The Templars passed on the secrets of alchemy to the Freemasons, who utilized them in the creation of the U.S. dollar.

It is not only on the present one dollar bill that the number thirteen has been used. On the early forty-dollar note (designed by Freemason Francis Hopkinson, who also designed the American flag, and the final version of the Great Seal of the United States), there was an explicitly Masonic symbol: a blazing altar out of which shot thirteen rays, burning underneath the All-Seeing Eye. On the first fifty-dollar bill, which Hopkinson also designed, there was the unfinished pyramid of thirteen layers, much like on the Great Seal, but it was more of a Sumerian-style ziggurat, or stepped pyramid, rather than a smooth-sided Egyptian-style pyramid, and there was no All-Seeing Eye. I also mentioned previously that the first pennies issued by the United States featured thirteen circles linked in a chain, along with the words "We are one." Coins minted by individual states included the symbolic number as well. Copper coins minted in Vermont in 1785 featured the All-Seeing Eye with twenty-six says shooting out (thirteen long, and thirteen short), interspersed with thirteen stars. In 1787, copper coins made in New York and New Jersey featured the eagle, the motto "E Pluribus Unum", and thirteen stars surrounding his head.

Incidentally, the use of the number 13 can be found not just on money itself, but throughout the very structure of the U.S. monetary system. For instance, there is the fact that there are exactly six types of coins, and seven denominations of paper money, currently in circulation in the U.S. Then there is the fact that the Treasury Department was created in 1789, exactly thirteen years after the birth of the USA in 1776. They even made a point of putting the date 1789 on the Treasury Department Seal in 1966, almost 190 years after the fact. The Treasury Seal, by the way, as I mentioned before, contains thirteen stars in its chevron.

The Federal Reserve has adopted the conspicuous use of the number as well. It was created in 1913. It consists of one Board of Governors overseeing twelve Federal Reserve Districts, and one central bank controlling twelve district banks, which in turn then control all of the member banks. The Federal Open Market Committee consists of twelve voting members: the seven members of the Board of Governors and five of the twelve Federal Reserve Bank presidents. Even the digits of the zip code for the Fed's headquarters in Washington, D.C., 20551, add up to thirteen.

One final piece of evidence brings the number 13, the US dollar, and alchemy together inextricably. To understand it, we must first look at how the number "13" can itself be a glyph representing the Hermetic caduceus, and the concepts behind alchemy. Just visually, you can see that "13" resembles a single-serpent caduceus broken down into its component parts: the "1" is the pole, and the "3" is the twisting serpent. In its original Arabic form, the three looked even more serpentine. The two glyphs, when put together, bring to mind the idea of a pole with an electric current running through it – an appropriate symbol, perhaps, of the constant flow of energy involved in alchemical processes. Or it could be thought of as an alchemical marriage of the passive, masculine "1" and the active, feminine "3." It could also be thought of as representing the ancient 3-in-one Trinity concept of God, the ultimate "E Pluribus Unum." The Templars most definitely were aware of Arabic numbers, so no doubt they were using "13" to express the idea of "thirteen" long before most others in Europe.

However, everything that I just said about the symbol "13" in the above paragraph could also be said about the "$" dollar symbol. In an earlier chapter I discussed the fact that the dollar sign was thought to have derived from the design used on Spanish silver dollars circulated in the American colonies, which featured the Pillars of Hercules wrapped in banners that said "Plus Ultra." But an earlier prototype of this design comes from coins made on the Phoenician island of Tyre, which feature both the Pillars of Hercules, *and* a serpent coiled around a tree, *ala* the Tree of Knowledge in the Garden of Eden. Look at the illustration (see figure 12). There is no doubt that the design of this coin is the ultimate origin of both the design on the Spanish silver dollar, and the modern "$" symbol. Ignatius Donnelly agreed, writing of this ancient Phoenician coin that:

... we have the Pillars of Hercules, supposed to have been placed at the mouth of the Mediterranean, and the tree of life or knowledge, with the serpent twined around it, which appears in <u>Genesis</u>; and in he combination of the two pillars and the serpent we have, it is said, the original source of our dollar mark.

The Tyrians provided much of the coinage used in ancient Israel, so these coins may very well have been in Solomon's treasury, and may have been discovered by the Templars as well. Of course, the Templars could have found these coins when they occupied Tyre during the Crusades. Indeed, it was one of the most important cities in the Latin Kingdom of Jerusalem, ruled over by the Templar Godfroi de Bouillon. Tyre was also was the site of some of the earliest Italian trading colonies, and thus was at the center of the rise of European mercantilism after the fall of the Templars. Tyre was a center of global trade for literally thousands of years, and played a pivotal role in many of the most important economic developments throughout history. How fitting, then, that this Tyrian coin apparently became the inspiration for the symbol of the American dollar, which would do more to transform the global economy than perhaps any other currency the world has ever known.

PART IV

Chapter Twenty-Two:
Spiritual Pyramid Schemes

So what exactly are the wise principles that have been passed down through the ages about how to create and grow wealth, or how to run an economy? Many of these principles are expressed in the Bible. The centerpiece of these teachings is the aforementioned concept of tithing. This idea is linked to a basic principle that has been around since ancient times - a principle dictating how blessings, either material or spiritual, can be multiplied by using an apparently effective although seemingly inexplicable spiritual law. This law states that a sacrifice made freely to any particular cause will be rewarded by God many times over. When applied to a priesthood, this means that the members of the congregation are rewarded for the tithes they give to the priests. The priests in turn give a portion of these tithes to the service of the god(s) they worship, and are in turn rewarded for that, mostly with more tithes. They also give a portion of the tithes they receive to the service of the community, and are rewarded for that as well.

This principle purportedly works not only for financial donations, but for any gift or service contributed freely to the cause. Thus, the priests are also rewarded for the spiritual services performed for their gods, such as prayers and rituals. It is a system in which any form of energy (of which money is certainly an example) can be fed into the system and multiplied exponentially. You could describe it as a spiritual pyramid scheme in which energy is channeled from the congregation to the priesthood, then from the priesthood to the god(s), where it is multiplied and then channeled back to the priests and the congregation. The rate of increase is often said to be times ten. Indeed, the word "tithe" means "tenth", since traditionally members of the congregation give a tenth of their annual income, expecting a ten-fold return, thereby creating a plenteous reserve for more tithes. Moreover, the priesthood traditionally uses a portion of the tithes for charity and community outreach, and thereby the priesthood itself earns a ten times increase of stored-up karmic rewards. So although the priests themselves may have taken a vow of poverty, the organization they serve can expand infinitely in wealth and power.

Thus the "Poor Knights of Christ of the Temple of Solomon", or the Knights Templar, who likewise took a vow of poverty, with the knights being required to give all of their property to the Order upon admittance. The Templars' poverty was symbolized by the icon of two knights riding on one horse, which they often used, implying that they doubled up on horseback to save the Order on its budget. (In fact, they had more than enough horses for whatever they needed. Each knight had at least one horse when he showed up to join.) The Order took the wealth donated to them by their members and patrons, then used it in various ways to multiply their wealth and power. They loaned money to kings and nobles throughout Europe, and thus not only earned interest, but gained influence over the very powerful figures who were indebted to them. The Templars also built magnificent castles and cathedrals throughout Europe, opened hospitals, and performed charitable work, spreading scientific and philosophical enlightenment throughout the lands they traveled. These charitable acts earned exponential rewards for the organization, according to the tithing principle previously discussed.

 The Church has used the tithes and spiritual energy of its followers to create a force that even today is the most powerful organization in the world, and once commanded an entire European empire. Like the Levites, Catholic priests take a vow of poverty, but the organization they serve is anything but poor. The Catholic Church's charitable activities remain unmatched, which undoubtedly earns them a great ongoing reward. This is how the Church has been able to create one of the most successful spiritual pyramid schemes in history. The Church laity pays with their love, worship, and money. In exchange they receive, at least once a week, a spiritual boon in the form of bread and wine - the blood and body of the deity - as well as the prayers of the priest, and the relief from the burden of sin after Confession. This temporary boon must renewed again the following Sunday, for the same price. The laity's gifts are then channeled directly back to Vatican headquarters, and the spiritual gifts are ultimately given to the deity who heads that organization. The financial gifts support the organization first, its activities second, and thirdly its active servants, the priesthood.

Chapter Twenty-Three:
The Law of the Harvest

But the Protestant Reformation did not end the practice of tithing for the breakaway Christian churches, or for the newly-formed churches which came afterwards. The Judeo-Christian tradition of tithing, as well as Christ's teachings on how God rewards charity (that "as ye sow, so shall ye reap"), have been the inspiration for a belief system touted by many modern Christian churches called "the Law of the Harvest." Basically it states the ideas which I have already reviewed: that the more you give to your church, the more God will reward you, financially and otherwise. *Deuteronomy 8:18* states: "...thou shalt remember the Lord thy God: for it is he that giveth thee power to get wealth." Thus many churches solicit donations from their members by calling these gifts "seed money", from which not only the church, but the giver's own bank account also, will purportedly grow. Sometimes, in exchange for these donations, churches take "prayer requests", promising to pray specific prayers on behalf of the givers, which God, it is promised, will answer as a reward for their donation.

One of the churches which has used this concept most effectively, although perhaps most ruthlessly, is one that is arguably fictitious: St. Matthew's Church, started by Reverend James Eugene Ewing. It operates out of a post office box in Tulsa, Oklahoma, even though Ewing, who is apparently the church's only minister, lives in California. Ewing has built over many years a hugely successful bulk mail operation. He sends out booklets to strangers targeted as living in low-income neighborhoods. The booklets are thick (almost 200 pages), artfully written, and lavishly illustrated, obviously constituting a considerable investment on the church's behalf.

The booklets explain how God's Law of the Harvest can be used to solve all of the ills in your life, and encourage the reader to join the St. Matthew's Church "Seeds of Success Gold Book Harvest Bible Plan." In exchange for regular gifts (seeds sown) to his ministry, Ewing will honor your prayer requests, and arrange the deals with God that you apparently have not been able to arrange for yourself. You will receive a "Harvest Book of Seeds", which Ewing describes as an "unusual book" that you must keep next to "your important papers such as your electric, gas and water bills", and that you should, "not fail to use it by sowing seeds to God towards your harvests out of each check." This book consists of coupons on which you write your prayer requests each time you "sow a seed" by giving Ewing a donation. Ewing also provides his church members with a magical "prayer rug" made of paper, and a "prayer coin" that is "a replica of those used in Bible days, featuring the head of Caesar." One might think that the purpose of this magical talisman is to remind you to "give unto Ewing that which is Ewing's", but he writes that its purpose is to "remind you that you have a financial partner, and that his name is Jehovah God!"

Ewing is understandably hated by such organizations as the Better Business Bureau, which only wishes that it had some legal basis for shutting his operation down. Although he references in his literature the "outreach work" that his church purportedly does, there is in fact no physical building that is St. Matthew's Church, only a post office box. The only official activity that the proceeds of is church are spent on is the printing and distributing of more literature about the "Harvest Plan." Ewing seems to have no shame, including in his booklet a prayer request form that you can fill out if you need a new automobile, complete with check boxes for the various brand options, ranging from Subaru to Rolls Royce. Despite his audacity, or perhaps because of it, Ewing's church has now earned tens of millions of dollars beyond its operating costs. Ewing is clearly a magus of the highest order, and seems to understand, in a very occult sense, the spiritual laws of financial success. His twelve-point outline of the Law of the Harvest is worth reviewing:

1. Your seed must be planted.
2. You must give your seed away to receive something.
3. You must plant what you expect to harvest.
4. Your harvest size is established when your seed is sown.
5. Your seed must be planted in good ground.
6. You must always wait a period of time between planting and harvesting.
7. You must maintain your crops for a proper harvest.
8. You must always sow to your harvest size, not from your harvest size.
9. Your expense is always highest at harvest time.
10. A part of your harvest is for sowing again.
11. A part of your harvest is for you to keep.
12. Your harvest is a miracle.

The essential Law of the Harvest has been, as I have explained, at the heart of religious traditions since ancient times. It has long been traditional for participants in a religious ritual to give a donation upon entering the church or ritual chamber. These donations not only serve to support the church or cult financially, but also serve as a reserve of spiritual energy donated by the participants to power the ritual. The concept is alluded to in the alchemical treatise *The Chymical Wedding of Christian Rosenkreutz.* In this story, the title character is invited to a royal wedding that is also an alchemical ritual. Before entering the castle in which the ceremony is held, he must purchase and then surrender to the gatekeeper a special gold coin that represents his donation to the household - the wedding gift. A plaque over the entrance to the castle reads "Date et dabitur vobis" - "Give and it will be given unto you."

Chapter Twenty-Four:
Alchemical Miracles

The principle of the exponential increase of money, or indeed of any form of energy, is similar to the idea of alchemy: of turning lead into gold, or the Prima Materia into the Philosopher's Stone. It means transforming the base into the lofty, by transforming energy from a lower form into a higher form. The alchemical stone can purportedly be made from any substance, even the most base, and then from it can be created anything which the heart desires, in inexhaustible abundance. This Philosopher's Stone is said to be so rare and valuable that one can use it to purchase anything in Heaven and Earth, even eternal life. As Christ taught, according to *Matthew 13:45-46*:

... the kingdom of heaven is like unto a merchant man, seeking goodly pearls: Who, when he had found one pearl of great price, went and sold all that he had, and bought it.

This symbolism links up with that of the Holy Grail in the Grail romances. Alternately described as either a cup or as a stone, the Grail is said to give abundantly whatever one wishes to receive. This it is able to do because, according to Wolfram von Eschenbach's *Parzival*, every year on Good Friday:

... one can infallibly see a Dove wing its way down from Heaven. It brings a small white Wafer to the Stone and leaves it there. The Dove, all dazzling and white, then flies up to Heaven again. Every Good Friday, as I say, the Dove brings it to the Stone, from which the Stone receives all that is good on earth of food and drink, a paradisal excellence - I mean whatever the earth yields.

Here we have an example of an alchemical transformation of quantity (high volume from a small volume, rather than quality (lead into gold). This is based on an alchemical principle well-explained by Albert Pike in *Morals and Dogma*:

...to make gold, we must first have gold. Nothing is made out of nothing; we do not absolutely create wealth; we increase and multiply it.

Someone who evidently mastered the art of creating very much from very little, as well as transmuting the base into the high, was Jesus Christ. He demonstrated this aptitude in several of his miracles, including that of the loaves and the fishes (in which a single serving of food was multiplied by thousands), and when he transformed water into wine at the wedding at Cana. He also returned to the concept repeatedly in his parables. In *Matthew 25:14-30*, Jesus explained the importance of investing one's money (or in a larger sense, one's energy) in something fruitful, in order to multiply it, rather than keeping it saved up, stagnate, unable to increase. He told his disciples the following parable. (Note: the word "talents" used here refers to a standard measure used to weigh precious metals, and thus it is here used as a monetary term):

For the kingdom of heaven is as a man traveling into a far country, who called his own servants, and delivered unto them his goods. And unto one he gave five talents, to another two, and to another one; to every man according to his several ability; and straightway took his journey.

Then he that had received the five talents went and traded with the same, and made them other five talents. And likewise he that had received two, he also gained other two. But he that had received one went and digged in the earth, and hid his lord's money.

After a long time the lord of those servants cometh, and reckoneth with them. And so he that had received five talents came and brought the other five talents, saying, Lord, thou deliveredst unto me five talents: behold, I have gained beside them five talents more. His lord said unto him, Well done, thou good and faithful servant: thou hast been faithful over a few things, I will make thee ruler over many things: enter thou into the joy of thy lord. He also that had received two talents came and said, Lord, thou deliveredst unto me two talents: behold, I have gained two other talents beside them. His lord said unto him, Well done, good and faithful servant; thou hast been faithful over a few things, I will make thee ruler over many things: enter thou into the joy of thy lord.

Then he which had received the one talent came and said, Lord, I knew thee that thou art an hard man, reaping where thou hast not sown, and gathering where thou hast not strawed: And I was afraid, and went and hid thy talent in the earth: lo, there thou hast that is thine. His lord answered and said unto him, Thou wicked and slothful servant, thou knewest that I reap where I sowed not, and gather where I have not strawed: Thou oughtest therefore to have put my money to the exchangers, and then at my coming I should have received mine own with usury. Take therefore the talent from him, and give it unto him which hath ten talents. For unto every one that hath shall be given, and he shall have abundance: but from him that hath not shall be taken away even that which he hath.

It seems strange that the Catholic Church would discourage usury, when here Jesus is explicitly encouraging it. He explains how loaning one's money upon usury creates an exponential increaser in wealth, and that it is not only righteous to do so, but slothful and wasteful not to.

In another biblical passage, *Mark 4:30 - 4:32*, Jesus used the imagery of a seed growing into a plant to demonstrate how something small can be multiplied into something great:

And he said, Whereunto shall we liken the kingdom of God? or with what comparison shall we compare it? It is like a grain of mustard seed, which, when it is sown in the earth, is less than all the seeds that be in the earth: But when it is sown, it groweth up, and becometh greater than all herbs, and shooteth out great branches; so that the fowls of the air may lodge under the shadow of it.

In *Luke 17:6*, Jesus turned the mustard seed parable into a statement on the power that faith (spiritual energy) can have, even in a small amount:

And the Lord said, If ye had faith as a grain of mustard seed, ye might say unto this sycamine tree, Be thou plucked up by the root, and be thou planted in the sea; and it should obey you.

Later, in *Luke 21 1-4*, Jesus explains how the worth (in spiritual value) of one's tithes is relative to the amount of wealth that one already possesses - in other words, that those who have much should give much. The text states:

And he looked up, and saw the rich men casting their gifts into the treasury. And he saw also a certain poor widow casting in thither two mites. And he said, Of a truth I say unto you, that this poor widow hath cast in more than they all: For all these have of their abundance cast in unto the offerings of God: but she of her penury hath cast in all the living that she had.

Chapter Twenty-Five:
A Commerce of Souls

In many ways, Judeo-Christianity is rife with financial metaphors. The entire religious system is about debt and payment. Adam created a deficit by sinning in the Garden of Eden, for which his descendants, the whole of humanity, must pay eternally in hellfire. Jesus purportedly paid off the debt by sacrificing his life, and Christians believe that we can all basically use the payment Christ made as a voucher to compensate for the debt we owe to God. This imagery of debt and payment in the sacrifice of Christ is enhanced by the fact that Christ's betrayer, Judas (who was the official treasurer of Christ's ministry) sold him to his murderers for thirty pieces of silver.

However, at least in traditional Catholicism, one cannot simply rely on the sacrifice of Jesus as a blanket payment for all sin. The way they see it is as sort of a "matching funds" system. If a person sins, they have to confess their sins to a priest, which is like submitting your debts to God for payment. By making your confession "in the name of Jesus Christ", you are calling into account the payment which Christ has already made to alleviate your debt. But the bit that Christ chips in is not the full payment, for the confessor must also perform certain acts in order to earn absolution: "Hail Marys", and the like.

In addition, the Catholic concept of Purgatory is linked to their idea of the "Treasury of Merit." In this view, there is a giant ledger in Heaven, kept by God, which keeps track of all of the liabilities created by the sins of Man. On the other side of the ledger are the assets earned by the good deeds of Man. At the top of this list is Christ's sacrifice, the largest deposit ever made into the Treasury of Merit. The Catholic Encyclopedia explains the concept of the Treasury as:

... the infinite riches obtained by the true merit of Christ's work on the cross. God freely grants us the privilege of contributing our own works to this Treasury. Catholics believe that the Holy Virgin Mary is the most important contributor next to Christ to the Treasury of Merit... This treasury is left to the keeping, not of the individual Christian, but of the Church. Consequently, to make it available for the faithful, there is required an exercise of authority, which alone can determine in what way, on what terms, and to what extent, indulgences may be granted.

The Encyclopedia also defines the term "indulgence":

The word indulgence ... originally meant kindness or favor; in post-classic Latin it came to mean the remission of a tax or debt. In Roman law and in the Vulgate of the Old Testament ... it was used to express release from captivity or punishment. In theological language also the word is sometimes employed in its primary sense to signify the kindness and mercy of God. But in the special sense in which it is here considered, an indulgence is a remission of the temporal punishment due to sin, the guilt of which has been forgiven.

One of the most controversial practices that the Catholic Church ever engaged in was the sale of indulgences. They actually put the remission of sins on sale for specific prices, for which the buyer would receive a certificate stating that his sins had been absolved. But more than that, a person could even post bail for his deceased relatives and spring them out of Purgatory - that uniquely Catholic concept borrowed straight from the works of Dante Alighieri, where a person who had died with a sin deficit (but who has not been condemned to eternal Hell) must pay penance in this "in-between zone" before entering Heaven. This became a very salable product with the congregation, and to push sales, the Church even came up with a catchy little jingle which went like this:

As soon as the coin in the coffer rings,
The soul from Purgatory springs.

It was this activity in particular which led Martin Luther to revolt against the Church and sparked what would eventually become the Protestant Reformation.

Chapter Twenty-Six:
A Mason's Wages

Like the Levite priesthood, the Catholic Church, and the Knights Templar, Freemasonry is yet another spiritual pyramid scheme. While the members do not take a vow of poverty, they do pay very high dues to the organization, and the Order in turn performs charitable works within the community. The idea of poverty is still symbolized, however, by the fact that Masonic initiates must present themselves divested of metal objects, especially coins, and barefoot, with their clothes disheveled. The emphasis in Freemasonry is not so much on the member's financial donations as it is on the member's contributions in the form of work. The primary symbolism used in their ritual is that of building, of putting one's skill and effort to work creating good things for God, Masonry, and the community. The members are then supposed to be rewarded for their work karmicly by the universe. Freemason Albert Pike wrote in *Morals and Dogma* that:

God is inexhaustible in his charity, as he is inexhaustible in his essence. That Infinite Omnipotence and Infinite Charity, which, by an admirable good-will, draws from the bosom of its immense love the favors which it incessantly bestows on the world and on humanity, teaches us that the more we give, the more we possess.

In fact, one Masonic ritual involves the initiate being paid his wages for working as a mason on the building of Solomon's Temple. Specifically they are paid the same wages –oil, wine, and corn (specifically the old use of the term "corn", which referred to wheat before the discovery of maize, now called "corn", in America) – which Solomon paid the Masons sent by Hiram of Tyre to help with the Temple, according to the Bible. Also, charity towards other Masons is emphasized in the order's rituals, and thus it is rightly believed that a mason will always favor another Mason in business if given the choice. This brotherly exchange of services between the members obviously gains each Mason, as well as the organization as a whole, a great deal of money and influence. That is why the Freemasons at one time had a considerable presence at the top of every Western government.

Albert Pike went on at length in *Morals and Dogma* about the Masonic idea of "earning wages", and the Masonic attitude towards business in general. Pike warned against attempting to reap too much profit from any business deal, and against using any deceitful means in business, even if such means are lawful. Any work which brings you gain to another man's detriment is, in Pike's view, only earning you a spiritual deficit which you will eventually have to pay for one way or another. He writes:

In intercourse with others, do not do all which thou mayest lawfully do; but keep something within thy power; and, because there is a latitude of gain in buying and selling, take not thou the utmost penny that is lawful, or which thou thinkest so; for although it may be lawful, yet it is not safe; and he who gains all that he can gain lawfully, this year, will probably be tempted, next year, to gain something unlawfully.

Let no man, for his own poverty, become more oppressing and cruel in his bargain; but quietly, modestly, diligently, and patiently recommend his estate to God, and follow his interest, and leave the success to Him.

Mr. Pike admonished Masons not to nitpick or negotiate overmuch about paying an employees wages, and told them never to break a promise, or contract, even if making that agreement turns out to have been a mistake. He also warns against making a promise you cannot keep, and against making private use of public property. He says:

Detail not the wages of the hireling; for every degree of detention of it beyond the time, is injustice and uncharitableness, and grinds his face till tears and blood come out; but pay him exactly according to covenant, or according to his needs.

Religiously keep all promises and covenants, though made to your disadvantage, though afterward you perceive you might have done better; and let not any precedent act of yours be altered by any after-accident...

Let no man take wages or fees for a work that he cannot do, or cannot with probability undertake; or in some sense profitably, and with ease, or with advantage manage. Let no man appropriate to his own use, what God, by a special mercy, or the Republic, hath made common; for that is against both Justice and Charity.

That any man should be the worse for us, and for our direct act, and by our intention, is against the rule of equity, of justice, and of charity. We then do not that to others, which we would have done to ourselves; for we grow richer upon the ruins of their fortune...

Pike is quite open here about his view that we will all be called into account for our spiritual deficit after death, and thus, it is better to store up treasures in Heaven rather than here on Earth. As he tells it:

It should be the earnest desire of every Perfect Master so to live and deal and act, that when it comes to him to die, he may be able to say, and his conscience to adjudge, that no man on earth is poorer, because he is richer; that what he hath he has honestly earned, and no man can go before God, and claim that by the rules of equity administered in His great chancery, this house in which we die, this land we devise to our heirs, this money that encircles those who survive to bear our name, is his and not ours, and we in that forum are only his trustees. For it is most certain that God is just, and will sternly enforce every such trust; and that to all whom we despoil, to all whom we defraud, to all from whom we take or win anything whatever, without fair consideration and equivalent, He will decree a full and adequate compensation.

Be careful, then, that thou receive no wages, here or elsewhere, that are not thy due! For if thou dost, thou wrongst some one, by taking that which in God's chancery belongs to him; and whether that which thou takest thus be wealth, or rank, or influence, or reputation or affection, thou wilt surely be held to make full satisfaction."

The wages earned by the word of a Freemason, then, are ultimately spiritual in nature, and can only benefit the Mason who receives them fairly.

Chapter Twenty-Seven:
The Mark of a Master Mason

The ceremony that goes along with the Masonic York Rite degree of "Mark Master" contains the most interesting details regarding the Masonic concept of "wages." In this ritual, the candidate is taught how to present his "mark" at the "warden's wicket" as proof of his worthiness to receive his wages. The "mark" is a personalized insignia, usually formed from the Mason's initials, which each candidate chooses for himself upon entering this degree. It must be unique to him, and he cannot alter it from that point on. The "warden's wicket" is a sort of bursar's window, through which the Mason to be paid thrusts his right hand, "with the thumb and first two fingers open, and the third and little fingers clenched, palm up", to quote *Duncan's Ritual of Freemasonry*, by Malcolm C. Duncan. With his clenched fingers he holds against his palm a small piece of paper on which is written his mark, face upward.

This serves as a secret code, a password, and only if the Mason presents his hand through the wicket in this way does the warden know that this man is truly a Mason, who has been "working in the Temple" and is thus deserving of a "wage." If the Mason presents his hand for payment without the mark, or without the secret hand signal, he is trying to commit fraud, the penalty for which is to have your hand cut off! At least, this is what the Mark Master candidate is told in the ritual when he first goes to the warden's wicket to receive payment, without having been told about the mark or how to present his hand.

After being threatened with amputation for doing it incorrectly, the candidate is scolded for his ignorance and told to choose a mark for himself. Once he does, the Senior Deacon comes towards him with a mallet and a chisel, purporting to engrave the mark onto the candidate's hand so that he will "carry it to the grave." Of course, in the end the mark is just written on a piece of paper and pressed against the palm of the hand. These sorts of empty threats of physical violence are as common to Masonic rituals are they are to college fraternity hazings.

When the initiate takes his oath for the degree, he is told to make a very peculiar promise. He says:

I promise and swear, that I will obey all regular signs and summonses given, handed, sent, or thrown to me from the hand of a brother Mark Master Mason, or from the body of a just and legally constituted Lodge of such, provided it be within the length of my cable-tow. Furthermore do

I promise and swear, that I will not wrong this Lodge, or a brother of this Degree, to the value of his wages (or one penny), myself, knowingly, nor suffer it to be done by others, if in my power to prevent it. Furthermore do I promise and swear, that I will not sell, swap, barter, or exchange my mark, which I shall hereafter choose, after it has been recorded in the book of marks, for any other one, unless it be a dead mark, or one of an older date, nor will I pledge it a second time until it is lawfully redeemed from the first pledge. Furthermore do I promise and swear, that I will receive a brother's mark when offered to me requesting a favor, and grant him his request if in my power; and if it is not in my power to grant his request, I will return him his mark with the value thereof, which is half a shekel of silver, or quarter of a dollar.

In other words, the initiate is promising to loan his fellow brethren money, or assist them in any other way possible, when a brother specifically comes to him for help by presenting his mark. It is his duty to grant the request if at all possible, but if it is not, he must return the mark to the other Mason, "along with the value thereof", which is "half a shekel of silver, or a quarter of a dollar." I suppose this means that if you cannot give the man exactly what he wants, you have to at least give him something. But the specific value of a mark as being half a shekel indicates that you are being charged a penalty for failing to meet your brother's needs.

If you are able to give him what he wants, then you are to retain his mark until such time as he is able to pay you back the amount loaned, or in some way return the favor. Some versions of the Mark Master oath even contain a stipulation in which the initiate swears not to grant that brother another favor until he has redeemed this mark. This means that each mason can only ask for one favor from one brother at a time, thus preventing abuse of the system. Of course, the new initiate learns that he too may use his mark to request a favor at any time in the future.

However, scarcely has the new Mark Master taken his oath when he is immediately presented with a mark and a request for 25 dollars from one of his brothers. This is all still part of the ritual. Having been divested of all cash, coins, and other "metal objects" before the rite, as is the tradition, the initiate has no money to give, and is prompted to say so, giving the presented mark back to the brother, but with no form of compensation to go along with it. For this, he is severely chastised by the Right Worshipful Master, who says:

How is this? Do you return it without the price, and thus break your oath before you rise from the altar? Have you not sworn, that where you could not grant a brother's request you would return his mark, with the price thereof, viz.: half a Jewish shekel of silver, or the fourth of a dollar? ...

Look further. Perhaps some good friend has, in pity to your destitute situation, supplied you with that amount, unknown to yourself: feel in all your pockets, and if you find, after a thorough search, that you have really none, we shall have less reason to think that you meant willfully to violate your obligation.

When the initiate searches his clothing, he indeed finds a quarter dollar coin there which one of the other brothers had placed there surreptitiously sometime during the rite. He then hands it over to the brother who has just presented him with a mark and a request. Upon doing this, he is given yet another lecture by the Right Worshipful Master:

Brother, let this scene be a striking lesson to you: should you ever hereafter have a mark presented you by a worthy brother, asking a favor, before you deny him make diligent search, and be quite sure of your inability to serve him; perhaps you will then find, as in the present instance, that some unknown person has befriended you, and you are really in a better situation than you thought yourself.

Later on in the same ritual, yet another lesson regarding Masonic wages is taught. The brothers in the room all pretend that they are workers in the building of Solomon's Temple again, and now it is "the sixth hour of the sixth day of the week." It is time to receive their pay for the week. But when they are each given a payment of one penny, the brethren erupt (as scripted) into vocal discontent, complaining that the new initiate is getting paid just as much as they, even though they have worked all week, and he has only just shown up. The Right Worshipful Master quiets the discontent by reiterating one of Jesus' parables, from *The Gospel of Matthew, 20:1-16,* which reads:

For the kingdom of heaven is like unto a man that is an householder, which went out early in the morning, to hire laborers into his vineyard. And when he had agreed with the laborers for a penny a day, he sent them into his vineyard. And he went out about the third hour, and saw others standing idle in the market-place, and said unto them, Go ye also into the vineyard; and whatsoever is right, I will give you. And they went their way. And he again went out, about the sixth and ninth hour, and did likewise; and about the eleventh hour, he went out and found others standing idle, and saith unto them, Why stand ye here all the day idle? They say unto him, Because no man hath hired us. He saith unto them, Go ye also into the vineyard, and whatsoever is right, that shall ye receive. So when even was come, the lord of the vineyard saith unto his steward. Call the laborers, and give them their hire, beginning from the last unto the first. And when they came that were hired about the eleventh hour, they received every man a penny. But when the first came, they supposed that they should have received more; and they likewise received every man a penny. And when they had received it, they murmured against the good man of the house, saying, These last have wrought but one hour, and thou hast made them equal unto us, which have borne the burden and heat of the day. But he answered one of them, and said, Friend, I do thee no wrong: didst thou not agree with me for a penny? Take that thine is, and go thy way: I will give unto this last, even as unto thee. Is it not lawful for me to do what I will with my own? Is thine eye evil, because I am good? So the last shall be first, and the first last; for many are called, but few chosen.

So the Mason is taught to accept his own proper wages rather then envying those of another. Finally, at the end of the ritual, the initiate is quizzed on certain "facts" regarding the Mark Master's degree. The quiz goes like this:

Q. By whom was this degree founded?

A. Our three Grand Masters - Solomon King of Israel, Hiram King of Tyre, and Hiram Abiff.

Q. For what purpose was it founded?

A. To be conferred upon all those who should be found worthy and well qualified, not only as an honorary reward for their zeal, fidelity and attachment to Masonry, but to render it impossible that any brother who should be found worthy of being advanced to this degree should ever be reduced to such extreme indigence as to suffer for the common necessities of life, when the price of his mark would procure the same.

Q. Who does a brother represent, presenting a mark and receiving assistance?

A. Our Grand Master, Hiram Abiff, who was a poor man, but for his regular and upright deportment, his great skill in architecture and the sciences, became eminently distinguished among the craftsmen.

Q. Who does a brother represent, receiving a mark and granting assistance?

A. Our Grand Master, Solomon, King of Israel, who was a rich man and eminently distinguished for his great liberality.

So here it is clearly states that the giving and receiving of charity and assistance within the lodge – the spiritual and monetary pyramid scheme of Freemasonry – is considered to be a continuation of a mutual benefit society created by King Solomon, Hiram of Tyre, and Hiram Abiff. The "wages" which Masonry deals in, then, are, in a metaphorical sense, riches from Solomon's treasury.

Chapter Twenty-Eight:
The Shekel-to-Dollar Exchange Rate

The fact that in Freemasonry, one's mark is specifically worth "one half-shekel of silver, or a quarter of a dollar" is very important. You will recall me mentioning previously that in ancient times all Jews were required to pay a temple tax of exactly one half-shekel. The shekel and half-shekel coins circulated in ancient Israel were all designed in Tyre, and many were minted there as well. Some of the later ones were made especially for the Israelite temple tax, and featured Judaic themes, but early on they were the same coins found in Tyre, with the same designs.

I suggested earlier in this book that the Templars may have discovered, either while stationed on Tyre during the Crusades, or while excavating beneath the Temple Mount, the ancient Tyrian coins which showed a serpent on a tree, the obvious origin of the dollar sign. It is even more likely that they became familiar with these Tyrian shekel and half-shekel coins also, each of which featured the bust of the god Melqart on one side, and an eagle on the other. These designs were strikingly similar to the designs found on modern American quarter-dollars, and on the large silver eagle dollars that used to be circulated in the US (see figure 28). Even more remarkable is the fact that Tyrian half-shekels were about the same size as American quarter-dollars. Considering that the Mark Master ritual clearly states that a half-shekel is equivalent to a quarter-dollar, the fact that the two coins are almost the same size, and carry almost the same design, is beyond coincidence.

Another observation I have made is that the size of the Tyrian full shekel coin, 31.5 millimeters, is almost the same size as each of the two roundels on the back of the US dollar bill which feature the front and reverse of the Great Seal. Using the Masonic formula of counting one quarter-dollar as a half-shekel, this means that there are (esoterically) two full shekels to the US dollar. I find it easy to believe that this formula, as a reference to the treasury of King Solomon, and the wages paid to the workers who built the Temple, was purposely incorporated into the US monetary system by the Freemasons involved in creating it. Hints about this secret principle are being given to us by the size, shape, and design of the currency.

Chapter Twenty-Nine:
Solomon's House - An Ongoing Project

It seems clear that the Freemasonic founders of the United States, as well as those who have helped to guide the development of the Republic well into the twentieth century, have organized the nation's institutions and operating systems along a pattern handed down, from one generation of initiates to another, at least from the time of King Solomon, if not further back in history. All of America's essential institutions, including, but not limited to, its economic institutions, are engineered in accord with the ancient spiritual principles that I have detailed in this book. The founding fathers of the U.S. may been so influenced by Enlightenment philosophy that they seemed "rationalist" and "humanist" in comparison to rabid Catholic and Protestant ideologues, but most of them were not materialists or atheists. They understood that everything which happens here on the physical plane has a corresponding effect in the spiritual realm, which in turn bounces back to affect the future of the physical plane, either positively or negatively, according to the original act. So the founders sought to create a Republic that would operate in such a way as to create maximum positive impact for both the citizens of the Republic, and the world abroad.

The principles of "spiritual pyramid scheme" - of an organization being used as an energy multiplier - apply to political states as well as secret societies. The citizens of a nation give not only their taxes, but also their faith, good will, and service to the institution which governs them. When that faith, goodwill and service is lacking, the nation become weak, but when it is abundant, the wealth and power of the nation increases exponentially. The leader of the nation, as its figurehead, must inspire and channel this faith and goodwill. The institutions of government are often specifically crafted to help him do this. With this in mind, the state makes use of faith-inspiring messages, and religious, heraldic, or occult symbolism in government insignias, or in the architecture of government buildings. For instance, many people know that certain streets and landmarks in Washington, D.C. are purposely laid out in the shape of a pentagram, and the theme is echoed by the nearby Pentagon, the center of the nation's military command. This iconography is used as an energy amplifier for the nation's goodwill and patriotism, to strengthen the spiritual power which the government needs in order to function.

Above all, though, the "Law of the Harvest" is demonstrated most purely in the operation of our capitalist economy, in which the investment of money, assets, and work is multiplied exponentially to the investor, the recipient, and to the economy as a whole, creating a machine-like system in which wealth is constantly multiplied as it is traded around amongst individual components of the system. As long as money continues to flow back and forth within the economy, it grows exponentially. When the movement of the money slows down, the growth slows down. It is considered a recession if the growth rate of the economy gets smaller, not just when the economy actually shrinks. This is because the economy is based not on a finite amount of gold or silver, but on energy that is constantly moving and constantly multiplying. This idea of the constant flow of money is at the root of our word "currency", as Jack Weatherford explains in *A History of Money*:

The frequent melting and reissuing of coins kept the mints at the Temple of Juno Moneta [in Rome] *in nearly continuous operation, whether the supply of gold and silver increased or not. The coins seem to have flowed out of the mint in a constant stream, and it is from the Latin word 'currere', meaning 'to run' or 'to flow', that the modern word 'currency' is derived, along with other, related words such as 'current' and 'courier.' The devalued coins gushed like a great river from Capitoline Hill through the entire empire.*

The image of a river of money constantly flowing out of Rome's Capitoline Hill may also be a partial explanation for the development of the term "capitalism." Although "capitol" and "capital" are spelled differently and have different meanings, they both come from the same root word, which, as I have said, means "of the head." This, I think, points to the true origin of "capitalism", as I think it refers to the head of Baphomet, which the Knights Templar believed "made them rich." As Michael Baigent and Richard Leigh said in *The Temple and the Lodge*, "No medieval institution did more for the rise of capitalism" than the Templars, and when they faded from the scene, they passed the responsibility for the development of capitalism first to the Italian merchants, then to the Freemasons.

Those are the ideological and spiritual roots of capitalism. But the economic seeds from which it sprouted – the "capital", if you will, used to fund the development of capitalism itself – came from the gold and silver looted by the Spaniards from the Americas. Gold objects were taken from the temples of Aztec and Mayan cults and melted down to make coins for Europe, while the Natives were enslaved to work in silver mines, to create even more coins for Europe. As I said before, this sudden influx of coinage into Europe sparked the Great Price Revolution, influenced the creation of corporations, and ultimately ended up in the coffers of the companies whose ventures in the New World created the North American colonies that became the United States. From there, Americans used the principles of capitalism, set down by Adam Smith in his book *The Wealth of Nations* in 1776 (the year of their nation's birth), to establish their own empire, and to transform the world. The fact that the American capitalist system was ultimately built using gold taken from the temples of conquered natives is an example of the same spiritual principle used by Constantine when he funded Constantinople with gold looted from pagan Roman temples. It is taking something consecrated to another purpose and sacrificing it to create something new. Such foundations constitute "seeds" from which the new temple, or new institution, is expected to grow, according to the ancient spiritual world-view.

A similar "seed planting" occurred, purportedly, when Jacques De Molay arranged for the Order of the Temple to be continued through a newly-created Masonic order. According to *The Occult Conspiracy: Secret Societies a – Their Influence and Power in World History*, by Michael Howard:

The survival of the Templar tradition was, according to historians, masterminded by the last Grand master, Jacques de Molay, while he was in prison. On the night before his execution de Molay sent a trusted confidant to the secret crypt in Paris where the bodies of the Order's Grand Masters were always entombed. This messenger took from the tomb various symbolic objects which were sacred to the Order, including the crown of the king of Jerusalem, a seven-branched candlestick from Solomon's temple and statues from the church which marked the site of the alleged burial place of Jesus.

De Molay told his trusted aide that the two pillars which stood at the entrance of the Templar tomb were hollow and contained large sums of money. He was told to use this wealth and the symbolic objects to recreate the Order so that its secrets would not be lost. The two pillars of the crypt's entrance were probably copies of the obelisks at the gateway of Solomon's temple. In addition to gold coin, the hollow pillars possibly contained manuscripts detailing the occult teachings of the Templar Order.

The idea of planting a spiritual seed and working, with the assistance of God, to cultivate it, is one also present in the tithing principles of the "Law of the Harvest" discussed earlier. When utilizing these principles during the foundation of something such as a new temple, it has long been customary to almost literally "plant a seed" in the foundation of the building, in the form of a cornerstone. As I have said, the cornerstone of Solomon's Temple was a sacred object used more than once in the Bible as a symbol of the divine, and it became a central emblem for the Freemasons as well. In the ancient Middle East, it was customary to consecrate new buildings by pouring a sacrifice to the building's patron deity onto the cornerstone – a sacrifice of oil, wine, and grain, the same set of items paid as wages to the masons who built Solomon's Temple. Again, these sacrifices were seeds. This is a tradition that the Freemasons have continued into the present time, as explained in a 1930 article called "Corn, Wine, and Oil" from the *Short Talk Bulletin* of the Masonic Service Association of the United States, where it says:

...corn, wine and oil - the produce of the land - are natural accompaniments to the dedication of a lodge which it is hoped will prosper, reap an abundance of the first fruits of Masonic cultivation and a rich harvest of ripe character from the seeds it plants.

...From earliest times consecration has been accompanied by sacrifice, a free-will offering of something of real value to those who thus worship. Hence the sacrifice of corn, wine and oil - the wealth of the land, the strength of the tribe, the comfort and well-being of the individual - at the consecration of any place of worship or service of God.

Like so much else in our ceremonies, the idea today is wholly symbolic. The Grand Master orders his Deputy (or whatever officer is customary) to pour the corn; the Senior Grand Warden to pour the wine, the Junior Grand Warden to pour the oil upon the 'Lodge' - usually a covered structure representing the original Ark of the Covenant.

At the founding of the American republic, there seems to have been no shyness at all about the fact that the country was being initiated as a Masonic institution. Many of the ceremonies which took place to consecrate the new nation, such as the swearing in of the first President, were openly Masonic rituals. George Washington took the Oath of Office dressed in Masonic regalia, with his hand resting on a Masonic Bible.

But the Masonic nature of these ceremonies most apparent than it was in the ritual installations of Masonically-consecrated cornerstones for the structures within the nation's new capitol, Washington, District of Columbia. The new city, named after the first President, was at once also a "district", named after the national goddess, Columbia. It was a truly Templar concept: the district was taken from the land mass of the states

of Maryland and Virginia. But once consecrated as "Washington, D.C.",
it was no longer part of Maryland or Virginia. It became an autonomous
region which was the seat of the sovereignty that governed the rest of the
states.

Washington, D.C. was originally laid out as a perfect ten-be-ten mile
square, oriented perpendicular to the compass. George Washington
picked out the land himself, and we might surmise that by choosing bits
of both Virginia and Maryland, he may have been making some allusion
to the Virgin Mary. According to David Ovason's *The Secret
Architecture of Our Nation's Capitol*, there are many allusions in the
architecture and layout of Washington, D.C. to the constellation Virgo.
This just confirms the idea that the nation was consecrated by its
founders to the ancient protectress of the state, the goddess Ishtar, or
Venus, under the name of "Columbia."

The foundation of the 100-mile-square grid that was originally
Washington, D.C. (before a chunk of it was conceded back to Virginia in
1848) made for a ceremony in itself, complete with the ritual laying of a
cornerstone in the traditional Masonic fashion. This took place at the
southern point of the grid, Jones Point, Virginia in 1791, and was
followed in 1792 by the laying of the cornerstone for the White House.
This was a ceremony again officiated by George Washington himself,
dressed up in his Masonic apron, and it actually took place on October
13, 1792 – the anniversary of the arrest of the Knights Templar. (It also
took place on the same day that the dollar was adopted as America's
official currency.) A Masonic ceremony occurred with the laying of the
cornerstone of the Capitol building in 1793, and with that of the
Washington Monument in 1848.

In each of these consecration ceremonies, the symbolic sacrifice of oil,
wine, and grain was poured upon the cornerstone. There can be no doubt
that this was a sacrifice made to God for the benefit of the new Republic
the Masons were creating. What better seeds to plant for the cultivation
of what the founders saw as a "New Atlantis", a "New Jerusalem", and a
"New Temple of Solomon"?

The United States as a whole appears to have been consecrated to three
different spiritual entities simultaneously. On the one hand, there is the
reverence clearly shown by America's founders to the God of the Bible,
also called Zeus by the Greeks and Jupiter by the Romans. The founders
made it clear in their phrasing of the Declaration of Independence, the
Constitution, the Bill of Rights, and in markings found on American

currency, that they considered the sovereignty of the United States to be "under God", guided by divine Providence. But there is also a clear reverence shown by the founders to the goddess represented by the constellation Virgo and the planet Venus, the Ishtar of the Babylonians, personified as Columbia, or Lady Liberty. Then in addition to this, we have the subtle but identifiable acknowledgment the founders apparently gave to the figure of Baphomet, a Templar and Masonic symbol of the Universal Agent which, in its Hermaphroditism, perhaps can be seen to represent a union of these masculine and feminine divine essences. We see a nod to the Baphomet in the explicit use by the founders of the number thirteen as a symbol of the Republic. There even seems to have been an effort to portray President Washington as a personification of Baphomet.

I am referring specifically to two depictions of George Washington made well after his death. In 1831, Congress commissioned a statue of the first President to go inside the Rotunda of the Capitol building (underneath the giant dome). The result that the sculptor came up with received a very negative reaction from the public. He had chosen to copy the appearance of a well-known Greek statue of Zeus. Washington appeared bare-chested and muscular, enthroned in a god-like posture, with a sword in his left hand, held by the blade, with the pommel sticking out. The statue's posture also hinted at the Eliphas Levi image of Baphomet, for his right hand pointed up towards the heavens, while the sword he held in his left hand pointed down toward the ground. I think the statue is great, but for some reason, it was universally scorned, and was finally removed from the Rotunda in 1962, consigned to the less conspicuous National Museum of American History.

It is claimed that the public bias towards this statue stemmed from the sentiment that it was inappropriate to depict an American President as a god. That was supposed to be even worse than presenting him as a king. But if this were truly a widely-held viewpoint, why was the painter Constantino Brumidi permitted to depict Washington in the exact same pose, sword and all, when he was hired to produce a fresco for the Rotunda of the Capitol building in 1875 – the Rotunda in which the supposedly hated and sacrilegious statue was already sitting? The name of this fresco (which is still there, by the way) is *Apotheosis of Washington*. The word "apotheosis" means, according to *Webster's Dictionary*, "the elevation of a person to the rank of a god." George Washington is shown here aloft in the clouds of Heaven, with the goddesses "Liberty" and "Fame" on either side of him, as well as thirteen virgins surrounding him in a circle.

There can be no doubt, considering the evidence presented in this book, that the foundation of the United States was a religious act – one which emboldened the fledgling republic to stand tall amongst the world's greatest powers, eventually exerting its own considerable influence upon them.

Chapter Thirty:
A Final Thought

I have covered the subject of the symbolic ritual sacrifices that were made during the foundation of America's capitol, Washington, D.C. These were seeds planted in hopes that the nation represented by Washington would prosper. But as we all know, it was not only this symbolic sacrifice that has made the United States great, but also those sacrifices of time, money, toil, and human life that her citizens and public servants have made throughout the years.

As a nation, America has sacrificed a great deal for the benefit of the world at large, and on a spiritual level, this has probably earned the country some of the rewards its citizens have enjoyed. Often criticized for being "the world's policemen", and for using its economic power to influence the politics of other nations, America has been, next to capitalism itself, the most successful instigator of positive change the world has seen. Although some may wish to concentrate on the negative effects of America's influence in various times and places throughout its history, an honest person would have to agree that, overall, the results have been good.

The US has given more aid to foreign countries than any other nation in history, and has used its military might to protect the weak from tyrants the world over. When it is necessary to destroy another nation in order to halt tyranny or to save the lives of others, the US always helps that nation to rebuild, and to create a better way of life than they had before. This is in stark contrast to the ancient tradition of pillaging, raping, and taking home the spoils of one's conquered enemy. Because of the military security that the United States is able to provide for many others abroad, these countries are then largely free from the burden of funding their own defense, and are often able to spend more money on social programs instead. The US tries to encourage freedom, equality, and prosperity everywhere that it can, and offers itself as a safe haven for the oppressed of the world. Some say America does too much. Others complain that she doesn't do enough. But America certainly does, at the present time, play the most pivotal role there is in maintaining the world's relative stability.

Why is it, then, that so many citizens who live in the greatest country in the world, and others abroad who have benefited from it, wish to see it torn down – to see all of this hard work, sacrifice, and carefully-planned cultivation brought to naught? For so many of these people, their hatred of the United States is based on fear of the American dollar, and the power that it holds. I believe that this fear stems from ignorance of the way in which money, and especially American money, truly works.

We have seen in our examination of history that money is, in itself, a radical idea, one that has developed over time to transform the world for the better, bringing, to the nations who used it properly, prosperity, technological advancement, and intellectual enlightenment. The best things in life may be free, but only when you have enough money to live comfortably do you have the freedom to enjoy those things. People who think that money cannot bring happiness have either never had enough money, or have always had plenty of it, and either way have not experienced the positive transformations that it can bring to a person's life. It can also, obviously, transform our society, and our environment, with seemingly limitless potential. To fear this power is to reject the most useful tool available to eliminate the evils and ills of our world. Before we can "make poverty history", we have get outside of the mindset of poverty.

I certainly hope, for the sake of our society, that people will being to educate themselves about money, and to learn to appreciate its magic.

APPENDICES

Appendix A:
The Tessera Hospitalis

The word "tessera" was a Latin word which originally meant "cube", and usually referred to small, square-shaped pebbles, marbles, or dice. It stems from the Greek word "tesseragonos", which means "four-cornered" or "square." A tessera hospitalis was a small token of friendship used in Roman antiquity, in which the item was broken in half, with one half being kept by each of the parties. If you met a new friend, especially while traveling, he might invite you to stay at his house for the evening. A tessera hospitalis would be broken between you before parting and, if you ever passed that way again, or if your new friend came through your neck of the woods at some point, even if it was many years later and you both looked different with age, you could compare the two tessera and rest assured that the other person was indeed the old friend you met so many years ago. The token also served as a pledge of hospitality for the future, to remind you of the good turn your friend once did you in the past, and of your duty to return the favor. Such objects exist even today. Schoolchildren sometimes share a token or metal, broken in half, which, when put together, reads "Best Friends."

Other tesserae were used for related purposes. A "tessera nummaria" was a voucher for a dole of money, used during the late Roman period when the government was giving out welfare money to its starving citizens. A "tessera theatratis" was a token used as a ticket to gain admission to a theater play. A "tessera militaris" was a token containing a password that was passed around amongst a division of an army. For this reason, the word "tessera" came to be a more general term meaning "password", as William Smith explains in his 1875 book, *A Dictionary of Greek and Roman Antiquities*:

A watchword was used at night and it consisted of a word or phrase that someone must say to prove that he was a bona fide member of a Roman unit or, if the authorized password was not used, he was considered an enemy. In the Roman army, the watchword for the night was not communicated verbally, but by means of a small rectangular tablet of wood upon which it was written. One man was chosen out of each of those maniples (common soldiers) and turmae (troop of cavalry containing thirty men, a squadron) that were quartered at that extremity of the lines most remote from the Principia. Each of these individuals (tesserarius) went near sunset to the tent of the tribune, and received from him a tessera, on which the password and also a certain number or mark were inscribed. With this he returned to the maniple or turma to which he belonged, and taking witnesses, delivered it to the officer of the next adjoining maniple or turma, and to the next until it had passed along the whole line. Then it was returned by the person who received it last to the tribune. The regulation was that the whole of the tesserae should be restored before it was dark, and if any one was found not returning the tessera at the appointed time, the row to which it belonged could be quickly discovered by means of the number or mark at the top, and so an investigation took place as to the cause of the delay, and punishment was inflicted upon the parties found to be at fault.

Not only mere passwords were circulated in this manner, but also, occasionally, general orders. Although the tesserarius received the tessera from the tribune, it proceeded in the first instance from the commander-in-chief and others. Under the Roman Empire it was considered the peculiar function of the prince to give the watchword to his guards.

From the application of this term to tokens of various kinds, it was transferred to the word used as a token among soldiers. This was the tessera militaris. Before joining battle it was given out and passed through the ranks as a method by which the soldiers might be able to distinguish friends from foes. Thus at the battle of Cunaxa the word was 'Zeus the Saviour and Victor', and on a subsequent engagement by the same troops, it could be 'Zeus the Saviour, Heracles the Leader.'

We can see now how the word "tiler", which originally referred to the person responsible for laying down tile floors in a medieval stonemason guild, came to refer to the officer in a Freemasonic lodge, whose job it is to admit people through the entrance, and to make sure that none but the appropriate lodge members enter. The words "tile", or "tessera", each could refer to both the tiles used on the floor, and the tokens or password presented to the tiler at the lodge as proof of membership. The fact that mosaics were made up of little tesserae, or tiles, put together, is at the origin of the word "tessellation."

It is funny, then, that while tesserae evolved into a form of money, the tessellated exchequer board became the common method of calculating money in medieval Europe. And along with the board, the exchequer would use small counting tokens, or tessera, called "tally chips" - "tally" being a word related to "tile", and to the "talis" in "tessera hospitalis." For "tally" comes from the Latin "talea", meaning "a cutting, rod, or stick", but it later came to mean "a thing that matches another", according to the Online Etymology Dictionary, etymonline.com. They state that the first such usage of this word was in 1651, can that it came from "practice of splitting a tally lengthwise, the debtor and creditor each retaining one of the halves." Also, the word "till" came to refer to a cash box.

But perhaps most interesting in this family of words is "talisman", which comes more directly from the Byzantine Greek word "telesma", the latter meaning "religious rite or ceremony", and also "payment or tax." Clearly this word must have developed from the practice of making a monetary donation in coin, or paying with something else and receiving a token as proof of payment, at the beginning or end of each ritual. The word "talisman" now generally refers to an enchanted object, usually a stone, wooden, or metal token, often engraved with religious or occult symbols, and used to transport the spiritual power of a spell or blessing. The object is usually imbued with the spell through a magical rite, and then a person either carries it with them as a charm, or gives it to the person they wish to cast a spell onto. I stated earlier in this book that I think all American coins and bills are talismans. This is what I mean.

Returning to the concept of the tessera hospitalis, it would seem that this may have influenced the Templar creation of the chit, or cheque. When you broke the tessera hospitalis in half, you created a unique pattern along the edge of each of the two pieces that was not likely to be replicated for forgery. This was the purpose of the cipher-encoded cheque system used by the Templars, and it is the same idea behind the netting or spider web patterns often used on modern checks and money – a pattern not likely to be replicated by those outside of the institution that created it. Like the tesserae hospitalis, modern checks and cash are essentially an "IOU" – a "promise to pay", made and accepted in good faith.

Appendix B:
The Wedjat Eye

We will now examine the Masonic symbol of the All-Seeing Eye, which can be found floating above the Egyptian-style pyramid on the back of the Great Seal of the United States. It has its roots in the Egyptian symbol of the left eye of Horus.

According to the story, the god Horus, son of Osiris, had his left eye destroyed by his nemesis, his uncle Seth. Later, the pieces of the eye were recovered, and put back together by the magician Thoth (the Egyptian equivalent of the Greek Hermes, and the Templar Baphomet). There was actually one piece that was not recovered, and that was the pupil of the eye. But this Thoth replaced himself through magic arts. His magical pupil was really the final piece which acted as the glue to hold all of the other pieces together. In this way, it was a bit like the keystone used in stonemasonry to hold together the pieces of an arch. The keystone takes on a great deal of symbolic significance in Masonic ritual, in which the rebuilding of Solomon's Temple is acted out, and there it is called "the stone that was rejected." It is ultimately a multi-layered symbol for the Philosopher's Stone, that hidden but nonetheless essential element which holds together physical reality.

The term "the stone that was rejected" is a line from the Gospels, in which Jesus is compared to a stone rejected from the building of Solomon's Temple that in the end becomes essential to the build. The fact that Masons use this term to refer to the keystone of Solomon's Temple is interesting, for in their own iconography, they show the keystone as holding together an arch which includes the pillars of Jachin and Boaz. Presumably, then, this arch is meant to represent the entrance to the Temple. And in the center of the keystone in this icon they sometimes place the All-Seeing Eye. This may connect on a metaphorical level with another symbolic eye - one which plays a significant role in Egyptian mythology, and which can definitely be said to have been "rejected": the eye of Ra, or "Atum-Re", their creator god. The story is explained by R.T. Rundle Clark in his book *Myth and Symbol in Ancient Egypt*, and takes place in the Abyss, or the primeval waters of creation:

Initially God seems to have only one Eye – a mysterious entity which is separable from its owner and which is sent out as an envoy to seek Shu and Tefnut [the first two human beings], who have become separated from Atum and are lost in the immensity of the Abyss. The Eye finds them and brings them back to their father, who proceeds to regenerate them as the life and order of the universe....

....The first pair were therefore not really existent until the Eye could return them to their creator. The Eye is personified might, the essential violence that is used to protect the gods and kings against disintegration in the waters or spirit enemies in the created world... the sending out of the Eye is equated with the Divine Word [of creation].

However, when the Eye returned, it found that on the head of Atum-Re the creator god, another Eye had grown in its place. The original eye became enraged with jealousy. To sooth its anger, Atum-Re had the eye transformed into a cobra, and then placed it on his head as a symbol of his royalty. Clark writes:

When it returned, it found that it had been supplanted in the Great One's face by another – a surrogate eye – which we can interpret as the sun or moon. This was the primary cause for the wrath of the Eye and the great turning-point in the development of the universe, for the Eye can never be fully or permanently appeased. The High God...turned it into a rearing cobra, which he bound around his forehead to ward off his enemies. This is why, on the terrestrial plane, the eye denotes the kingship of the pharaohs in terms of sheer power, while cosmically it is the 'sovereign eye' and burning heat of the sun.

Thus the Egyptian cobra crown was born, while the Eye symbol came to be known by the epithet, "the Royal Eye of Gopta", the latter word being the original form of "Egypt."

In each of these myths, the eye seems to be a symbol of the restoration of order from chaos. The pieces of the eye of Horus get made whole by Thoth, and the eye of Ra leads God's creation back home from the waters of the Abyss. Indeed, the eye symbol did become part of an Egyptian hieroglyph which meant "order." It was formed by an eye over an arch with two pillars (see figure 35), just like in the Masonic icon previously described, and it stood for the word "Mayet", or "Maat", which meant "order", but also "wisdom", just as the "met" does in "Baphomet." According to Egyptologist E. Wallis Budge, a more simplified eye hieroglyph meant "to create, to make, to fashion, or to produce."

However, the eye of Horus was a very particular symbol, and it had a very particular name: "udjat", or "wedjat." It was drawn in a very specific way, and it included a strange little curly-cue, seemingly shaped like a Fibonacci spiral, jutting out of it at the bottom right. But this is the most amazing part. Just as the eye was reassembled from its various parts, the symbol of the wedjat eye could be disassembled into its various parts, each of which then came to represent a mathematical fraction of the whole. These parts of the eye became in themselves little symbols that served as numbers representing fractions. Specifically, the whole eye was supposed to contain 63/64. One piece symbolized 1/2, another 3/4, then 1/8, 1/16/, 1/32, and 1/64. But there were only 63/64 in the whole eye. The missing 1/64 did not really exist in the physical realm. It represented the pupil of the eye made from the magic of Thoth, which held the rest of the eye together. It makes sense, then, that one could only take the eye apart and use the individual pieces for numbers if the pupil was not there holding the pieces together (see figure 34).

In Egypt, the wedjat symbol was the ultimate measurement from which all of their other forms of measurement were made, much like the dimensions of the perfectly cubic Holy of Holies of the Tabernacle, and later, Solomon's Temple, were used as the basis of measurement in Israel. For this reason, a system of weights was assigned based on the 63/64 of the wedjat eye. This became the method for not only weighing out bundles of wheat and other goods, but also for the weighing out precious metals, and the assigning of values to coins, especially silver ones. So the Egyptian monetary system (which was only used at short periods in its history) was based on the different parts of the wedjat eye too. The eye also became a symbol for the act of religious sacrifice, and tokens featuring the wedjat eye were used as vouchers for those who had made donations to the temple priesthood.

The different parts (and progressive fractions) of the wedjat eye are believed by anthropologists and historians to have been originally based on the phases on the moon. This is part of the reason why Thoth, who put the eye back together, is thought to be a lunar deity. This is interesting, considering that the wedjat eye may be related to another item which involved lunar symbolism: the chessboard. Modern chessboards of course have 64 squares to them, just as the wedjat eye ultimately has 64 parts, and the chessboard is ringed by 28 squares, representing one lunar cycle, with the white and black squares implying alternating periods of day and night. In this vein, an Egyptian depiction of the wedjat eye floating over a chessboard-style tessellated pattern has been found that is quite noteworthy (see figure 36).

We should also note that the number 64 is a cube of 4. The "perfect cube" is a symbol very important to Freemasons and other occult groups. Not only was the Holy of Holies in the Tabernacle (and later the Temple) perfectly cubic, as well as the "New Jerusalem" described in the *Revelation of St. John the Divine*, but so also is the Philosopher's Stone of the alchemists said to be cubic. The goat-headed Baphomet is often shown seated on a cubic stone. But more pertinent to out current examination is what the Templar offshoot group the Priory of Sion has to say about the "perfect cube." In one of their well-known published documents, called *Le Serpent Rouge*, the mysterious author refers to the process of reassembling the "scattered stones" of the "perfect cube", using the Masonic "square and compass." Interestingly, this is their poem that is arranged in the form of a 13-house zodiac, implying a lunar calendar, and makes several reverences to the game of chess.

Because of its association with money in Egypt, I have often wondered if the word "wedjat" could be related to other monetary words like "chit", "check", "jack", or "shekel." It seems almost certain, though, to be related to the word "watch", which not only means "to see or observe", but also "to measure" or "to check" (as in "watchword", a term identical to "password." It is probably also related to the Hindi word for "eye", which is "ajna." It could even be related to "agio", a financial term I will explain in Appendix D.

However, the name "udjat" was also, along with "Gopta", at the root of the place-name "Egypt", for according to E. Wallis Budge, the Egyptians sometimes called their own land "Utcha", thus identifying "the name of Egypt as the country of the Eye of Ra", as Budge put it.

Appendix C:
The Bohemian Connection

The examination in Appendix B of the word "wedjat" and its possible relationship to the word "check" brings to mind a tantalizing, though perhaps unlikely, possibility. "Check" is of course identical to the word "Czech", used to describe a person from Czechoslovakia, a land that used to be called "Bohemia." Czechoslovakia is supposedly named after the man, "Czek", who, according to legend, founded the land. He was purportedly a nomadic wanderer and trader, who, at one point in his travels, rather haphazardly stopped on a hill and decided that he and his entourage would live there from then on. The people of the area gained a reputation for being nomadic and rather untrustworthy traders, so "Bohemian" became a slang term for such people (although it is now a more redeemed term for somebody who is eccentric). The word "Bohemia" is said to come from an ancient Celtic tribe called the "Boii" who once lived in the area. But as for "Czech", because of the Templar association with travel and commerce, I cannot help but wonder if the word "chit" used by the Templars may have influenced the name.

I mentioned earlier in this book that the word "check", or "chit", was most probably related to the word "jetton", a type of coin, also invented by the Knights Templar, used as a reckoning counter in conjunction with the exchequer board. Incidentally, the term "jetton" has sometimes been applied by chroniclers to another form of coin used during the medieval period, which were more properly called "abbey tokens." Thomas Wright described their purpose in *Worship of the Generative Powers*:

Antiquaries have given the name of abbey tokens to a rather numerous class of such medals, the use of which is still very uncertain, although there appears to be little doubt of its being of a religious character. Some have supposed that they were distributed to those who attended at certain sacraments or rites of the Church, who could thus, when called up, prove by the number of their tokens, the greater or less regularity of their attendance.

A number of such "abbey tokens" minted by Templar preceptories have been found, bearing none other than the goat-headed, hermaphroditic image of the Baphomet. These were possibly used either as a reward token to prove a knight's attendance at a Templar ritual, or as a ticket proving his right to be at the ritual.

In his book *The Arcane Schools*, occultist John Yarker explains the employment of abbey tokens by certain Gnostic sects that venerated John the Baptist. These tokens would be used as an admission ticket for cult members attending a Gnostic mass. Yarker compares the tokens to the Roman tesserae, and acknowledges that some of them were minted by Templars. As he puts it:

The Gnostics adopted the Apostle John as their Patron; his symbol was the Eagle, or bird of the sun, which was the Sectarians' sacred emblem; it is found in Egypt at the foot of the tau cross, and now on the jewel of a Rosy-cross Mason. The Gnostic tokens were a sectarian version of the older pagan 'Tesserae hospitalis,' on which was the head of Zeus ... There can be no doubt that the Arcane Discipline had them as tokens of preparation for the Supper of the Lord; many, if not all, the Catholic confraternities present a token which is generally worn under the clothes from a ribbon. Some of the tokens yet preserved belonged to the Templars, and there are a quantity of Abbey tokens, which are struck in lead or pewter with the cross on one side, and on the obverse a variety of designs.

Very pertinent to our current discussion is the fact that, according to the eighteenth-century Austrian scholar Joseph, Baron von Hammer-Purgstall, Templar abbey tokens depicting the Baphomet have been found in the Bohemian (now Czech) towns of Mureau, Prague, and Egra. Indeed, the Templars had quite an influence in Bohemia, as well as the Teutonic Knights, and the "Knights of Johann", the local Knights Hospitaller, because Bohemia was the site from which the Third Crusade was initiated by Emperor Frederick Barbarossa. But it is hard to ignore the fact that the Czech flag and arms make use of the chequer pattern, perhaps tying it to the Templars. In addition, it is host to the town of Janvov, which mean's "John's family", as well as Joachimstal in the Jachymov valley, where the first silver dollars were mined and minted. "Joachimstal", you will recall, means "Joachim's Valley." The name "Joachim" is just another way saying "Jachin" – the name of one of the pillars from Solomon's Temple. Also, given the apparent influence in the area of the cult of John, we should note again that "Jack" is a slang term for "John." We find names based on "John" or "Jack" all over the modern Czech Republic.

Just as the term "bohemian" became a slang term for a nomadic trader, a swindler, and a cheat, so too did the term "gypsy." *Webster's Dictionary* defines the word as, "a member of a traditionally itinerant people, originally of North India, now residing mostly in permanent communities in many countries of the world... [It stems from] gipcyan, variant of

Egyptian, from the belief that Gypsies originally came from Egypt." Like the Bohemians, the Gypsies have a historical association with the Templars. In their book *The Temple and the Lodge*, Michael Baigent and Richard Leigh documented a protective relationship between the Knights Templar families resident in Scotland, and the Gypsies there, whom the Templar families saved from persecution on more than one occasion. They even organized esoteric mystery plays with a group of Gypsies on the groups near Rosslyn Chapel.

Gypsies were so known for their dishonest business deals, including the sale of bogus psychic readings, magical spells and herbal remedies, that the word "gyp" came to be slang for theft or fraud. Interestingly, there is yet one more group who, like the Bohemians and the Gypsies, became so known for this behavior that their own group's name became an adjective for "nomadic swindler", and "stranger"; the Chicanos, Mexican immigrants to the United States. This concept must be at the root of the word "chicanery", from the French seventeenth century term "chicanerie." According to *Webster's* Dictionary, this word means "the use of sly or evasive language, reasoning, etc., to trick or deceive"; and, "a tricky or deceitful maneuver, subterfuge." Note, again, that the root word "Chic" is, much like "Czech." Perhaps it is related to the fact that "jack" is a slang term for theft also.

One more thing that ties these groups together is this: the Templars, the Bohemians, and the Gypsies have all been credited by various historians with helping to import from the East the deck of playing cards, and from there to have helped it developed into the Tarot deck, called by modern occultists the "Book of Thoth." The alchemist Papus even specifically referred to it as "the Tarot of the Bohemians." And Masonic writer Albert Pike wrote that the alchemical Azoth was "the same as the Thoth of the Bohemians."

Appendix D:
Goat Money

Relevant to the facts and theories discussed in Appendix C, I note the following: The word "Gopta", which both "Egypt" and "Gypsy" derive from, is also, according to antiquities expert L.A. Waddell, at the root of the words "Gothic", "goetic" (which means "magical"), and "god." He ultimately traced it to the Sumerian word "kad", which means "lord" or "king." He also thought that "kad" was at the root of the word "goat", because the ancients had many gods that took the form of a goat. As we know, the Templar idol Baphomet had a half-goat form, as did the Greek inventor of alchemy, Hermes.

The goat-headed Baphomet drawing of Eliphas Levi has now morphed into our stereotypical depiction of Satan, and modern Satanists have adopted him as one of their symbols. The icon they use for him is an inverted pentagram with the details of a goat's face drawn into it – an image which is also based on a drawing by Eliphas Levi. They call this symbol the "Goat of Mendes", linking Baphomet to the goats that were used for fertility rites at the temple of Ammon, in the ancient Egyptian city of Mendes. In these rites, the goat copulated with the temple priestesses, an appropriately sinister heritage for a Satanic symbol.

In addition to being important to Templars and to modern Satanists, goat symbolism plays a peculiar role in the lore of Freemasonry. This subject was discussed in great detail by British Master Mason Eugene W. Plawiuk in his essay *Liber Capricornus: The Symbol of the Goat*, where he writes:

Our first experience upon entering the Lodge as apprentices is to be warned about the Goat. Even before we are informed of 'in whom we should put our trust', we are given knowing looks followed by such comments as; 'He's going to get the Goat', or 'You are going to ride the goat', or even 'Look out for the Goat.' It is a good thing that we are informed that we place our trust in God, since some poor unfortunate entered apprentice could understandably be forgiven for replying; 'In the Goat.'

The origin of this humorous initiatory jest about the Goat is shrouded by the veils of time. Several older brethren I have conferred with seem to have no idea of where or when it originated. It could have originally been imported from America by that practical joker and fellow Mason; Benjamin Franklin...

207

Mr. Plawiuk then goes on to describe how Masonic researchers have in the past equated the goat symbol with the idea of building temples, and that it can be connected to the Masonic term for God: "The Great Architect of the Universe", for which they use the anagram "G.A.O.T.U." As Plawiuk explains it:

What a better symbol to attribute to our own striving to understand the G.A.O.T.U. then a Goat? And here too we find an anagram for 'Goat.'

According to a research monograph on the Dionysian Artificers and Early Masonry edited by Manly P. Hall, the symbolism of the Goat relates to the pre-Christian God Pan, Dionysius. The Goat-God was accepted by the later Greek Mystery Schools as the symbol of the Temple Builders. ...

Elsewhere, Mr. Plauwiuk analyzes similarities between the Scapegoat of *Leviticus* and the Masonic myth of Hiram Abiff, the architect of Solomon's Temple who, according to the legend, was murdered by his own apprentices for refusing to reveal to them the "secret" of the Temple.

I have already discussed the symbolism of Zeus' she-goat wet nurse, Amalthea, whose skin he made into his magical shield, the Aegis, while its horn became the Cornucopia. "Aegis" means "goat skin", as the root word "aeg" means "goat" in Greek. Goats were very important to the Greeks, for they ate goats' meat, made milk from their cheese, and used their skin for clothing. This is why the Aegean Sea, which lent its name to their entire civilization, has its roots in this syllable, "aeg."

Interestingly, goat skin is one of the earliest forms of money or currency, used long before coins were invented. Also, in ancient Rome, they had an abacus system for settling monetary accounts, in which discs carved from goats' horns were used, in a manner similar to the way jettons were used in the later European exchequer system. And in modern times, the term "goat money" is used to refer to high-quality counterfeit bills. This term has apparently evolved from a more general usage in which it referred to any money earned by unusual means. Perhaps this explains the rarely-used word "agio", which refers to profit gained from currency exchange, or the difference between a coin's face value and the value of its metallic content.

Of even greater interest was the word "bucks", which is, of course, is a modern slang term for American money. But it originated as a gambling term used to denote poker chips. *Webster's Dictionary* defines it as "an object used by a poker player as a marker for who has the deal, for the ante, etc." It can also be used as a verb meaning "to gamble, play, or take a risk against", or "to strive or compete for." This is related to the term "to buck the odds", and also the act of bucking; that is, "to resist or oppose obstinately"; or "to force a way through or proceed against an obstacle"; or "to strike with the head, or butt." This is related to the actions of animals, including goats, whose young are called "bucks." These animals often "buck", as in "to leap with arched back and land with head low and forelegs stiff." Also, the skin of these animals is tough enough to act as a "buckler", or shield. Indeed, Zeus' Aegis was a buckler, and it was literally made from buckskin. One of *Webster's Dictionary*'s definitions of "buck" was simply "buckskin." The hide of a goat itself could be referred to as "buck."

Appendix E:
The Jack in the Box

As an aside related to Appendix D, I would like to note that the word "bucks" could also have been influenced by the source of the word "box." This ultimately comes from the Latin word "pyx", which originally was a general term for any square container. This is why there is a star constellation called "Pyxis", in the same cluster as Argo and Columba. In fact, Pyxis is the mariner's box inside the Argo ship. But over time, the word "box" took over the more general meaning, while "pyx" retained two very specific definitions.

The first definition of "pyx" is, according to *Webster's Dictionary*, "The box or vessel in which the reserved Eucharist or Host is kept" for Communion in a Catholic church. This practice of keeping the host inside a pyx led in a strange way to the development of the term "jack-in-the-box." It was originally a term of derision used by Protestants to make fun of the idea that the Communion wafer actually contained the body of Christ. It implied that it was not Christ, but a "jack", or demonic spirit, which inhabited the wafer These associations are still present in the modern children's toy called the "jack-in-the-box", which expresses the idea of a magical imp living inside of a box, like a genie in a bottle.

Based on its association with the Protestant-perceived illusory nature of the Communion and Eucharist rites, the phrase "jack-in-the-box" evolved. As Robert Nares wrote in his 1905 *Glossary of Words, Phrases, Names, and Allusions*, by 1570, jack-in-the-box referred to a thief "who deceived tradesmen by substituting empty boxes for others full of money." The term could also refer to substitute items placed in the box to fool the victim further. Thus, "jack" came to refer to counterfeit money, and also to the act of theft or fraud. This is yet more evidence of a relationship between the words "jack" and "check", for in those times it was always necessary to "check" your money box after completing a deal, to make sure you had not gotten "jacked."

This brings me to the second modern definition of the word "pyx", again according to *Webster's Dictionary*: "a chest or mint, in which specimen coins are reserved for trial by weight and assay." This definition, referring to the testing of coins to see if they have been counterfeited or debased, stems from around 1350, the post-Templar era in which Italian mercantilism was beginning to spring up. The "Pyx Chamber" at Westminster Abbey in London was also built in the 1300s, for the same purpose. There the tools and records of the national Exchequer were kept, along with boxes of coins that awaited the "Trial of the Pyx", a public demonstration of the purity of the metal content in the nation's currency.

Appendix F:
Casting a Fortune

Returning to the subject of gambling discussed in Appendix D, I find it peculiar that the term "casting a fortune" is always associated with divination, but the word "fortune" can also mean "luck" or "good chance." Yet the word "fortune", when used by itself, is associated with wealth. This is, in a sense, fitting, since chance, represented by the Wheel of Fortune, is the essential element in some forms of divination, as well as in gambling, which is always an attempt to gain wealth. Thus, many techniques used in divination are also used for gambling. Many of the same elements used in divination can also be used for conjuration, or casting a spell. It would seem that "casting a spell" and "casting a fortune" may at one time have meant the same thing.

I discussed previously that playing cards were the inspiration for the Tarot. Each card in the Minor Arcana of the Tarot corresponds to a playing card, and before Tarot was even invented, playing cards were used in a form of divination known as "cartomancy." Furthermore, both playing cards and chess are thought to have evolved from a game played in ancient India (now modern Afghanistan) that involved both a chessboard, and tokens made out of animal skin which resembled modern playing cards. The game was played mainly for gambling purposes. These things are discussed in greater detail in my article "Work with the Square and Compass", which was published in the book *The Arcadian Mystique: The Best of Dagobert's Revenge Magazine* (Dragon Key Press, 2004).

The Catholic Church has traditionally prohibited gambling games, mainly because, in the ancient world, the tokens used in the games often represented gods that were invoked for good luck, and the pieces were believed to be enchanted with Satanic spells. Playing cards in particular were anathema, due to their association with divination. Both Tarot and playing cards were referred to by the Church as "the Devil's picture books."

But long before the Roman Church banned gambling, the licentious and pagan Rome of antiquity did also, for the simple reason that the men of the city had become so obsessed with it that they could no longer be persuaded to engage in useful work. The practice was banished to the week-long festival known as Saturnalia, beginning on December 22, which is, interestingly, the onset of the astrological period of Capricorn – the house of the Goat. (I should note here that the Federal Reserve was created at the beginning of Saturnalia, on December 23, 1913.) During this festival, the participants would each wear a conical Phrygian hat, which they called a "liberty cap." This hat was traditionally worn by slaves who had been freed, but in this instance it symbolized a Roman citizen's freedom to indulge himself in gambling and other pleasures during Saturnalia. The liberty cap was later taken on as ritual garb by the Bavarian Illuminati, a politically radical French Masonic offshoot created in 1776, the same year as the American Revolution, and believed by some historians to have influenced the French Revolution. "Liberty cap" is now the name of a type of psychedelic mushroom

Although the Romans banned gambling except during Saturnalia, they did not succeed in curtailing it completely. Before these games had been played in the streets, but when they were banned, many players simply formed private men's clubs, and moved the gaming tables indoors. These clubs often had special passwords for admittance, and oaths of secrecy for the members. The association between gambling and secret societies has persisted throughout history. Gambling was a vice which the Knights Templar were known for. Even today, poker nights are one of the most commonly held events at Masonic lodges and other private men's clubs. It is also popularly associated with more sinister, underworld organizations like the Italian mafia, as mobsters often own or control gambling casinos.

Appendix G:
The Root of All Evil

Pertaining to Appendix F, the truth, in part, is that gambling has historically been considered sinful because money itself has always had infernal connotations. Even in the pre-Christian era, before the love of money was declared "the root of all evil" by Jesus, the desire for much gold and silver was always thought to be the worst form of greed, a deadly sin. The concept of money has been associated since ancient times with figures which we would now consider to be synonymous with the Devil. The Roman god of the underworld, Plutus, was also the god of wealth, and was depicted on coins holding a cornucopia. Also, recall the message of Freemason Johann Wolfgang von Goethe's *Faust*, a play about a man who sells his soul to Satan in exchange for the ultimate wisdom. One of the bits of wisdom which the Devil gave to the title character was the secret to alchemy, which in this instance turned out to be the printing of paper fiat currency.

Today, spells to acquire money make up the majority of the activities engaged in by modern Satanists and neo-pagans, and like Faust, they often attempt to sell their souls in order to gain it. Even the Queche Indians of the Bolivian Andes, who work in the silver mines there and were converted to Catholicism long ago, still perform sacrificial offerings to the Devil and his wife, whom they call "El Tio" and "China "Supay", in order to earn monetary rewards. They mainly sacrifice cigarettes, alcohol, and cocaine to their demonic idols, earning, they believe, small and random boons of cash from the universe. To get the big payoffs, they say, you have to sacrifice an animal or a human, and only the *real* Devil-worshippers do that. This, they believe, is how their corporate bosses got to own the silver mines that these Indians slave in every day. To them, the association between money and the Devil is intrinsic, for they see cash as still being tied to gold and silver, which are mined from the Earth's fiery nether regions – the Devil's domain.

In the Bible, the invention of metallurgy is credited early on in *Genesis* to the figure of Tubal-Cain. He was among the accursed race of Cainites, descended from the world's first murderer, Cain, who murdered his own brother. Thereafter, he was cursed to be a "fugitive and a vagabond" for the rest of his days. Cain himself was the inventor of agriculture, described in *Genesis* as "a tiller of the ground." His name, which appears in the histories of many other ancient Semitic cultures besides the Hebrew, has contributed to the formation of words in English and other languages that mean "grain", "corn", "bread", or "cane." But in Hebrew,

"Cain" meant "to acquire, to create, to fashion, to produce, or to accomplish" – much the same meaning that the Egyptians gave their wedjat eye. When used as a noun, it meant "smith"; that is, "one who makes things." Thus it seems easy to say that "Cain" is at the root of the word "coin." For in addition to being a noun indicating a metallic token, "coin" can also be used as a verb, meaning "to invent." The noun "coin" is derived from the verb definition, for a coin is an object that has been "coined."

Both Cain and his descendant Tubal-Cain are portrayed in Judeo-Christian literature as evil geniuses, too smart for their own good. There is something sinister about their accomplishments (the invention of agriculture and metallurgy), and of their selfish desire to create things, no matter how wonderful those creations may be. This is fitting, for in the same *Book of Genesis* in which the story of Cain appears, we read about two other seemingly positive acts: the obtaining of ultimate wisdom from the Tree of Knowledge (Adam and Eve in the Garden of Eden), and the building of a magnificent tower leading to Heaven (the Tower of Babel). Both of these acts were portrayed in the Bible as sins punishable by death. The message of *Genesis* (a word that means "creation") is that creating things is God's job, not Man's and therefore mankind has no need to learn the principles of creation. This was a Judaic concept that the Catholic Church took and ran with, adding in its own new rules restricting free thought, science, and learning, which they considered to be threatening. In this world-view, at the extreme end of it, the invention of money could be seen as one of man's most audacious acts: creating something and declaring it to have a particular value, from which the value of everything else in the world can be measured. So it makes sense that money itself would seem inherently deviant in the traditional judgment of Catholicism. In a way, money is inherently a Faustian symbol of Man's rebellion against God in his quest for more knowledge of the world and control of his surroundings.

The other biblical passage which most clearly associates money with evil is found in *The Revelation of St. John the Divine, 13:16-18*, where this prophesy is made regarding the Antichrist:

And he causeth all, both small and great, rich and poor, free and bond, to receive a mark in their right hand, or in their foreheads: And that no man might buy or sell, save he that had the mark, or the name of the beast, or the number of his name. Here is <u>wisdom</u>. Let him that hath understanding count the number of the beast: for it is the number of a man; and his number is <u>Six hundred threescore and six</u>...

Curiously, 666 is the exact number of talents of gold that King Solomon gained in tribute every year, according to *II Chronicles 9:13*. It is strange that he would receive exactly this many talents every year, rather than different amounts each year. Also, why such an odd number? And why does the text make a point of mentioning this particular number? Finally, why does the passage in *Revelation* state, prior to giving the number 666, that "Here is wisdom"? And why, after explicitly saying that this is the "number of the beast", does it then immediately also state that it is the "number of a man"? Could it be referring to the wisdom which the man King Solomon used to expand his fabled treasury? Could the number 666 somehow be a key to this wisdom?

Either way, the description here of needing a mark on one's hand in order to conduct business certainly brings to mind the aforementioned "Mason's mark" which, in the degree of Mark Master, must be pressed against your palm (and is symbolically engraved there) before you can receive your wages for helping to build Solomon's Temple. (In the real world, historically, stonemasons have engraved such personalized marks onto each brick they crafted, to identify their work.) While needing to have a mark on your hand in order to get paid may not itself be evil, St. Paul of Tyre reminds us in *Romans 6:23* that "the wages of sin is death."

Appendix H:
The National Treasure

In the 2004 movie *National Treasure*, the proposition is put forth that the Freemasons who founded the United States possessed the treasure from Solomon's Temple, as well as a large number of other treasures from around the world, which they had inherited from the Knights Templar. Supposedly they secreted this vast cache, mostly of gold, in a gigantic underground vault beneath the Trinity Church on Wall Street in New York.

In the film, the protagonist, Benjamin Gates (played by Nicholas Cage), discovers the treasure, which is shown to include tons and tons of gold, worth billions of dollars, by following clues left on the back of the Declaration of Independence, as well as other places. But the process necessitates that he break a number of U.S. laws along the way. By the time he finds the treasure vault, he has already been captured by the police, and must make a deal with them in order to avoid a prison sentence. The negotiation is led by a policemen named Sadusky (played by Harvey Keitel), who, like Gates, is a Freemason. They end up making a gentleman's arrangement in which Gates agrees to give ninety percent of the treasure to the world's museums, while keeping ten percent, or the value thereof, for himself. Sadusky suggests that this is what the Masonic founders of America would have wanted, in the spirit of Masonic charity. In the final scene of the film, it is revealed that the discoverers of the treasure have only accepted one percent of the treasure's total value in compensation, rather than ten percent. So they were even more charitable to the world than they were required to be.

Clearly, this film contains a morality tale regarding the Freemasonic ideals of charity, and the concept of "a Mason's wages." The tithing concept is implied by the suggestion that the protagonist should keep only ten percent of the treasure. Specifically, it was more of a "reverse tithe", encouraged in some protestant churches today when a person has been particularly blessed by the Lord, and they are so wealthy that they can afford to give ninety percent of their income to the church. In this case, the characters reverse-tithed to the world on behalf of the United States, using the treasure of the Knights Templar, which includes the treasure of Solomon's Temple. It is implied cryptically in the film that this treasure was the original capital, the seed money, upon which the wealth of America is based. Why else would the screenwriter choose to locate the fictional treasure in a vault beneath Wall Street – the nation's main financial district?

Bibliography

Baigent, Michael, and Leigh, Richard. *The Temple and the Lodge*. New York, NY, USA, 1989.

Baigent, Michael, Leigh, Richard, and Lincoln, Henry. *Holy Blood, Holy Grail*. New York , NY, USA,1982.

Baigent, Michael, Leigh, Richard, and Lincoln, Henry. *The Messianic Legacy*. New York, NY, USA 1986.

Barker, Sheila. "Poussin, plague, and early modern medicine." *The Art Bulletin*. http://www.looksmartcollege.com/p/articles/mi_m0422/is_4_86/ai_n858 3707 (December, 2004.)

Barnstone, Willis. *The Other Bible: Ancient Alternative Scriptures*. New York, NY, USA, 1984.

Blavatsky, H.P. "Animated Statues." *Theosophical Articles: Reprinted from <u>The Theosophist</u>*. USA, 1982.

Boase, T.S.R. *Kingdoms and Strongholds of the Crusaders*. London, UK, 1971.

Buchholz, Todd G. *New Ideas From Dead Economists: An Introduction to Modern Economic Thought*. New York, NY, USA, 1990.

Budge, E.A. Wallis. *From Fetish to God in Ancient Egypt*. New York, NY, USA, 1988.

Butler, Alan, and Dafoe, Stephen. *The Warriors and the Bankers: A History of the Knights Templar from 1307 to the Present*. Belleville, Ontario, Canada, 1998.

Cain, Tubal. *Secrets of the Lodge: Origins, Practices, and Beliefs of Freemasonry*. Denbighshire, Wales, UK, 1999.

Cajori, Florian. *A History of Mathematics*. London, UK 1919.

Cassaro, Richard Russell. *The Deeper Truth: Uncovering the Missing History of Egypt*. New York, NY, USA, 2000.

The Catholic Encyclopedia, http://www.newadvent.org/cathen/ (2005.)

"Corn, Wine, and Oil." (Author unknown.) *Short Talk Bulletin - Vol. 8. August 1930, No. 8.* Published by the Masonic Service Association of the United States. http://www.phoenixmasonry.org/cornwine.htm. USA, 1930.

Clark, R.T. Rundle. *Myth and Symbol in Ancient Egypt*. New York, NY, USA, 1959.

Cooke, Jean, Kramer, Ann, and Roland-Entwistle, Theodore. *History's Timeline*. London, UK, 1977.

De Vere, Nicholas. *The Dragon Legacy: The Secret History of an Ancient Bloodline*. San Diego, CA, USA, 2004.

Donnelly, Ignatius. *Atlantis: The Antediluvian World*. New York, NY, USA, 1976.

Duncan, Malcolm C. *Duncan's Ritual of Freemasonry*. USA, 1976.

Ewing, James Eugene. *Divine Help*. Tulsa, OK, USA, 2000.

The Federal Reserve website, http://www.federalreserve.gov/ (2005.)

Ginzberg, Lewis. *The Legends of the Jews, Volume IV: From Joshua to Esther*. Portland, OR, USA, 2005.

Goldman, Benita. "Byzantium and Her Arts." Eastern Michigan University. http://www.emich.edu/abroad/staff/Benita/Byzantine.html. 2005.

Goodwin, Jason. *Greenback: The Almighty Dollar and the Invention of America*. New York, NY, USA, 2003.

Greider, William. *Secrets of the Temple: How the Federal Reserve Runs the Country*. New York, NY, USA,1987.

Hall, Manly P. *The Lost Keys of Freemasonry*. Canada, 1976.

Hall, Manly P. *The Secret Destiny of America*. Canada, 1991.

Hall, Manly P. *The Secret Teachings of All Ages: An Encyclopaedic*

Outline of Masonic, Hermetic, Qabbalistic and Rosicrucian Symbolical Philosophy. USA, 1971.

Hamilton, Edith. *Mythology: Timeless Tales of Gods and Heroes.* New York, NY, USA,1969.

Hauck, Dennis William. *The Emerald Tablet: Alchemy for Personal Transformation.* New York, NY, USA, 1999.

The Holy Bible: King James Version. Grand Rapids, MI, USA, 1989.

Howard, Michael. *The Occult Conspiracy: Secret Societies a – Their Influence and Power in World History.* Rochester, VT, USA, 1989.

The Jewish Encyclopedia, http://www.jewishencyclopedia.com/ (2005.)

Knight, Christopher, and Lomas, Robert. *The Hiram Key: Pharaohs, Freemasons, and the Discovery of the Secret Scrolls of Jesus.* MI, USA, 1996.

Landes, Richard. *Relics, Apocalypse, and the Deceits of History: Ademar of Chabannes, 989-1034.* USA, 1998.

Lietaer, Bernard. *The Future of Money: Creating New Wealth, Work and a Wiser World.* USA, 2001.

Lunn, Martin. <u>*Da Vinci Code*</u> *Decoded.* New York, NY, USA, 2004.

"The Mandylion, Descriptive Information." (Author unknown.) The website of the Printery House Conception Abbey. http://www.printeryhouse.org/mall/Icons/Portraits/a12.asp (2005.)

Mayer, Martin. *The Fed: The Inside Story of How the World's Most Powerful Financial Institution Drives the Markets,* USA, 2001.

McCormick, W.J. McK. *Christ, the Christian, and Freemasonry.* Belfast, Ireland, 1984.

McIntosh, Christopher. *The Rosicrucians: The History, Mythology, and Rituals of an Esoteric Order.* York Beach, MN, USA, 1997.

Morrison, Paul.*The Poetics of Fascism: Ezra Pound, T.S. Eliot, Paul de Man.* Oxford, UK, 1996.

National Treasure. Disney Films, USA, 2004.

Online Etymology Dictionary, http://www.etymonline.com/ (2005.)

Ovason, David. *The Secret Architecture of Our Nation's Capitol: The Masons and the Building of Washington, D.C.* New York, NY, USA, 2000.

Ovason, David. *The Secret Symbols of the Dollar Bill*. Harper Collins, New York, NY, USA, 2004.

"The Pentagram." (Author unknown.) From the website of the Masonic Grand Lodge of British Columbia and Yukon. http://freemasonry.bcy.ca/anti-masonry/pentagram.html. 2005.

Pike, Albert. *Morals and Dogma*. Richmond, VA, USA, 1927.

Pinkham, Mark Amaru. *Guardians of the Holy Grail: The Knights Templar, John the Baptist, and the Water of Life*. Kempton, IL, USA, 2004.

Plawiuk, Eugene W. *Liber Capricornus: The Symbol of the Goat*. Presented to Norwood Lodge No.90 A.F.& A.M. G.R.A. http://www.freemasonrywatch.org/baphomet.html September 3, 1991.

Rest, Friedrich. *Our Christian Symbols*. Philadelphia, PA, USA, 1959.

Rithchie, John. "The Templars, The Shroud, the Veil and the Mandylion." *Templar History Magazine*. http://www.templarhistory.com/mandylion.html (1999-2004.)

Schaff, Philip. *The Nicene & Post-Nicene Fathers Of The Christian Church, Second Series, Volume II*. New York, USA, 1997.

Schneider, Michael S. *A Beginner's Guide to Constructing the Universe: The Mathematical Archetypes of Nature, Art, and Science*. New York, NY 1994.

Shugarts, David A. *Secrets of the Widow's Son: The Mysteries Surrounding the Sequel to* The Da Vinci Code. New York, NY,USA, 2005.

Simpson, D.P. *Cassell's New Latin Dictionary.* New York, NY, USA, 1959.

Smith, Adam, *The Wealth of Nations.* USA, 2003.

Smith, William. *A Dictionary of Greek and Roman Antiquities.* USA, 1973.

Still, William T. *New World Order: The Ancient Plan of Secret Societies.* Lafayette, LA, USA, 1990.

The Treasury Department website, http://www.ustreas.gov/ (2005.)

Twyman, Tracy R. (Ed.). *The Arcadian Mystique: The Best of Dagobert's Revenge Magazine.* Portland, OR, USA, 2004.

Twyman, Tracy R. *The Merovingian Mythos and the Mystery of Rennes-le-Chateau.* Portland, OR, USA, 2004.

Von Eschenbach, Wolfram. *Parzival* (excerpt). From *Transformations of Myth Through Time: An Anthology of Readings.* Orlando, FL, USA, 1990.

Waddell, L.A. *Egyptian Civilization: Its Sumerian Origin and Real Chronology, and Sumerian Origin of Egyptian Hieroglyphs.* USA, 1930.

Waite, Arthur Edward. *The Rider Tarot Deck.* Stamford, CT, USA, 1971.

Weatherford, John. *The History of Money.* New York, NY, USA, 1997.

Webster's Collegiate Dictionary. New York, NY, USA,1999.

Wilford, John Noble. *The Mysterious History of Columbus: An Exploration of the Man, the Myth, the Legacy.* USA, 1991.

Wright, Thomas. *Worship of the Generative Powers: A History of Phallic Worship.* USA, 2001.

Yarker, John. *The Arcane Schools.* USA, 1997.

About the Author

Tracy R. Twyman is the former Editor of *Dagobert's Revenge Magazine*, and has been researching the occult history of the West for over a decade. She is the author of *The Merovingian Mythos and the Mystery of Rennes-le-Chateau* (Dragon Key Press, 2004), and the editor of *The Arcadian Mystique: The Best of Dagobert's Revenge Magazine* (Dragon Key Press, 2005). She lives in Portland, Oregon with her husband, Brian, and her cat, Martin.

DRAGON KEY PRESS

Catalogue
2005/2006

DRAGON KEY PRESS
PO BOX 8533
PORTLAND, OREGON 97207
USA

DRAGONKEYPRESS.COM

THE MEROVINGIAN MYTHOS
AND THE MYSTERY OF RENNES-LE-CHATEAU
By Tracy R. Twyman

A taste from the Tree of Knowledge...

- What exactly was the artifact known as the "Holy Grail"?
- Was civilization created by beings that were greater than human?
- Was there once a primeval language given to us by the gods?
- Does the so-called "Grail bloodline" descend not just from Jesus, but from the biblical Cain?
- What is it that makes the "Grail bloodline" special, and gives the "Grail kings" a divine right to rule?
- Do five mountains in Southern France contain the greatest treasure of human history?

Occult expert and historian Tracy R. Twyman has been investigating the enigma of the Holy Grail and Rennes-le-Chateau for more than seven years, and has written extensively about it in *Dagobert's Revenge Magazine*, as well as other publications. Now at last she has fully disclosed the shocking conclusions of her exhaustive research.

The Merovingian Mythos
And the Mystery of Rennes-le-Chateau
By Tracy R. Twyman, ISBN # 0-9761704-0-X
6 x 9" - 237 pages , **$19.95, Item # 001**

THE ARCADIAN MYSTIQUE:
THE BEST OF DAGOBERT'S REVENGE MAGAZINE
Edited by Tracy R. Twyman

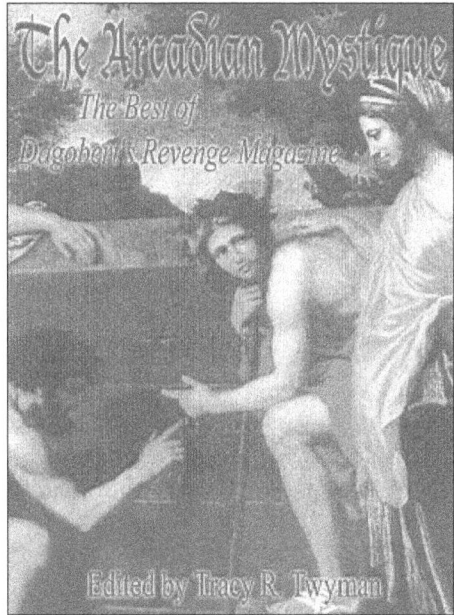

Since 1996, *Dagobert's Revenge Magazine* has been a beacon to those seeking the light of the Holy Grail. Powerfully written, exhaustively researched, and totally unique, *Dagobert's Revenge* was the first and only magazine devoted to the emerging phenomenon of neo-Arcadian culture, breaking ground on many modern occult subjects. Mounted on a white horse poised for the future, *Dagobert's Revenge* has resolutely heralded the Arcadian Age. And now, the best articles from hard-to-find back issues are available in one volume, as well as articles never before printed. This is a treasure chest of invaluable arcane wisdom. Articles include (but are not limited to):

- *The Prieure de Sion: A Star-Studded Cast of Grand Masters*
- *What the Hell is the Holy Grail?*
- *Baphomet: The Severed Head that Wouldn't Die*
- *The Real Meaning of 'Et in Arcadia Ego'*
- *The Celestial Sea and the Ark of Heaven*
- *Dead But Dreaming: The Great Old Ones of Lovecraftian Legend*
- *Jean Cocteau: Man of the Twentieth Century*
- *Pax Europa: The United States of Europe*
- *Call Me Ishmael: The Biblical Roots of the Persian Gulf Conflict*
- *The Choice Vine: Mary Magdalene*
- *The Judas Goat: The 'Substitution' Theory of the Crucifixion*

The Arcadian Mystique:
The Best of Dagobert's Revenge Magazine
Edited by Tracy R. Twyman, ISBN # 0-9761704-2-6
8.25 x 11" - 258 pages, **$24.95, Item # 002**

DAGOBERT'S REVENGE MAGAZINE
VOLUME 5, NUMBER 1
Edited by Tracy R. Twyman

Volume 5 #1 was the final issue of this much-loved niche periodical dedicated to the mysteries of the Grail and Freemasonry. Articles include:

Between the Swastika and the Cross of Lorraine: The Ambivalence of the Priory of Sion During World War II.

Le Hieron du Val D'Or, from *Secret Dossiers, by Henri Lobineau. (Translated from the original French.)*

The Daughter of God: The Real Story of Joan of Arc.

The Occult Roots of Christianity.

The Divine Couple.

Giants on the Earth.

Work with the Square and Compass: The Hidden Mysteries of Chess and Playing Cards.

Geometric Revelations: An Interview with Henry Lincoln.

Chaldean Genesis: The Secret Legacy of the Architect-Priests.

And more...

Dagobert's Revenge Magazine
Volume 5, Number 1
Edited by Tracy R. Twyman, ISBN # 0-9761704-1-8
8.5" x 11" - 80 pages, **$5.95, Item # 003**

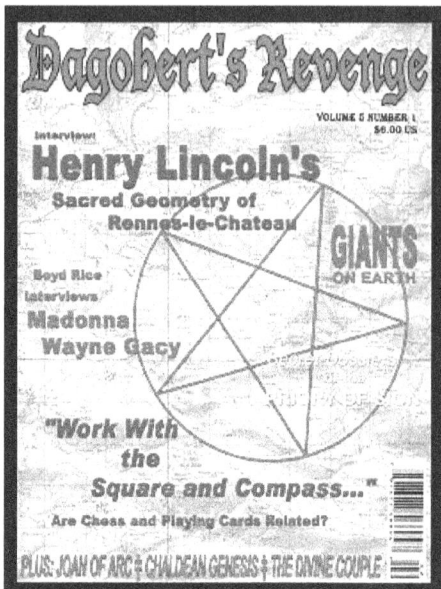

THE STORY OF "MORMONISM", AND, THE PHILOSOPHY OF "MORMONISM"
By Dr. James E. Talmage

Read the early history and beliefs of the one of the most peculiar, and fastest growing, religious movements of our time, told from the point of view of another time. *The Story of 'Mormonism'* tells the captivating biography of the movement's founder, the tumultuous tale of their westward migration, and the unending conflicts that occurred along the way. *The Philosophy of 'Mormonism'* tackles many of the more controversial traditions of the Church of Latter-Day Saints, from polygamy, to celestial marriage, to ancestral baptism, with sensitivity and insight.

The Story of 'Mormonism' is a revised and reconstructed version of lectures delivered by Dr. James E. Talmage at the University of Michigan, Cornell University, and elsewhere. The *Story* first appeared in print as a lecture report in the Improvement Era, and was afterward issued as a booklet from the office of *The Millennial Star*, Liverpool. In 1910 it was issued in a revised form by the Bureau of Information at Salt Lake City, in which edition the lecture style of direct address was changed to the ordinary form of essay. The third American edition was revised and amplified by the author. The subject matter of *The Philosophy of 'Mormonism'* was first presented as a lecture delivered by Dr. Talmage before the Philosophical Society of Denver. It appeared later in the columns of the Improvement Era.

The Story of 'Mormonism'
and
The Philosophy of 'Mormonism'
By Dr. James E. Talmage, ISBN # 0-9761704-3-4
6" x 9" - 65 pages, **$9.95, Item # 004**

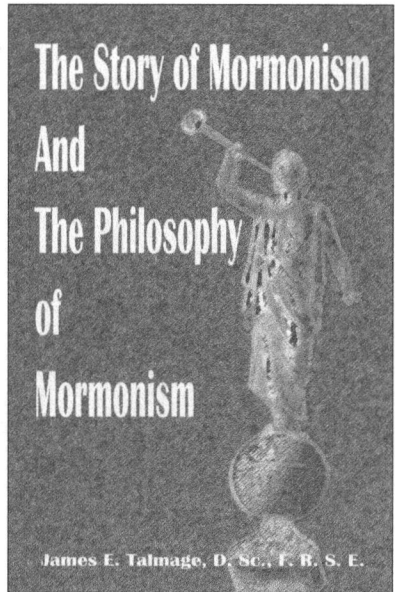

THE LEGENDS OF THE JEWS, VOLUME IV:
BIBLE TIMES AND CHARACTERS
FROM JOSHUA TO ESTHER
By Louis Ginzberg

This series of books, published between 1909 and 1939, was certainly the first, and is perhaps the greatest, comprehensive overview of Judaic tradition, belief and lore ever published. Utilizing his proficiency in the Latin, Greek, Syriac, Aramaic, Arabic and Akkadian languages, Ginzberg was able to draw not only from the Torah, Talmud, and Midrash, but also from the Pseudepigrapha, Christian scripture and apocrypha, and Islamic legends, his sources spanning in origin from three centuries before Christ until his own modern times. The present volume, which has been out of print for some time, pertains to matters stretching from the time they entered the Promised Land, under the commanding lead of their anointed ruler, Joshua, until the rule of Queen Esther, including the period of the Judges, the reign of kings Solomon and David, the dividing of the kingdom, the captivity, and the return from exile. Aside from the scriptures themselves, few writings have had as much impact on modern Jewish thought, and on the popular conception of Judaism, as Louis Ginzberg's *Legends of the Jews*.

The Legends of the Jews, Volume IV:
Bible Times and Characters From Joshua to Esther
By Louis Ginzberg, ISBN # 0-9761704-5-0
6" x 9" - 219 pages, **$19.95, Item # 005**

THE UNKNOWN LIFE OF JESUS CHRIST
By NICOLAS NOTOVITCH

The Unknown Life of Jesus Christ was origi- nally published in 1894 by its author, the Russian-born and well-traveled aristocrat, Nicolas Notovitch. It consists of a lengthy and entertaining account of his travels throughout India and Tibet, where he met a number of lamas who insisted that accord- ing to their folk legends, Jesus Christ had once visited their land. By sheer chance, Notovitch claimed, he broke his leg during his journey, and was taken to a monastery to recover for a few weeks. It was there that he was able to acquire a copy of the sacred Tibetan scripture, *The Life of St. Issa: Best of the Sons of Men*, which was translated by Notovitch and is reproduced in this volume, followed by an analysis of the text from the author. According to the text, Jesus spent his early years from age 12 to 29 (the so-called "lost years" not recorded in Christian scripture) travel- ing throughout India and Tibet, learning from the local religious leaders, until he was driven out through persecution by the ruling castes for chal- lenging their authority. Although held by some to be a forgery, No- tovitch's "discovery" sparked a series of books by other authors on the subject of Jesus in the Orient that were published in the early half of the twentieth century, and the concepts which he introduced have now be- come staples of modern mystical thought.

The Unknown Life of Jesus Christ
By Nicolas Notovitch, ISBN # 0-9761704-4-2
6" x 9" - 95 pages, **$9.95, Item # 006**

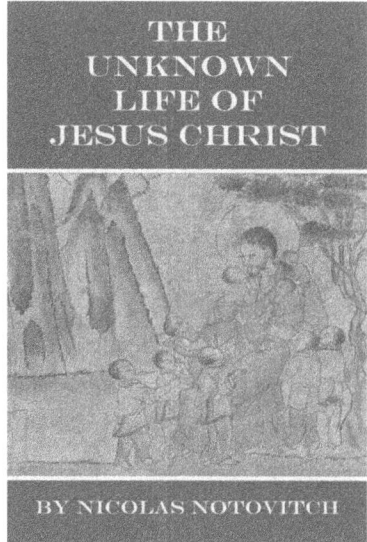

To order any of the items in this catalogue, cut out the order form on the following page, and write in which items you are requesting. The price of each item is listed with its catalogue entry. For shipping to the U.S. or Canada, please add $4.30 for the first item, and $1.00 more for each additional item. For shipping to all other countries, please add $8.55 for the first item, and $1.00 more for each additional item. Send this in, along with your check or money order, to:

DRAGON KEY PRESS
PO BOX 8533
PORTLAND, OREGON 97207
USA

Or you can shop online at:

DRAGONKEYPRESS.COM

Also check out our website for tons of free articles, and our blog, *Plus Ultra*, updated daily.

ORDER FORM

ITEM DESCRIPTION OR NUMBER	QTY.	PRICE	EXT. TOTAL
		$	$
		$	$
		$	$
		$	$
		$	$
SUBTOTAL			$
SHIPPING: *US AND CANADA - $4.30 FOR THE FIRST ITEM - ADD $1.00 PER ADDITIONAL ITEM ALL OTHER COUNTRIES - $8.55 FOR THE FIRST ITEM - ADD $1.00 PER ADDITIONAL ITEM*			$
TOTAL ENCLOSED			$

NAME

ADDRESS

CITY   STATE   ZIP

COUNTRY

MAKE CHECKS AND MONEY ORDERS PAYABLE TO:

DRAGON KEY PRESS
PO BOX 8533 ✝ PORTLAND, OREGON 97207 ✝ USA

OR SHOP ONLINE AT
WWW.DRAGONKEYPRESS.COM

www.ingramcontent.com/pod-product-compliance
Lightning Source LLC
Chambersburg PA
CBHW021900020426
42334CB00013B/408

9 7 8 0 9 7 6 1 7 0 4 6 4